CHRISTIAN FAITH IN FOCUS

CHRISTIAN FAITH
IN FOCUS

by

Gordon J. Spykman

BAKER BOOK HOUSE • GRAND RAPIDS, MICH.

Library of Congress Catalog Card Number: 67-29071

ISBN: 0-8010-7907-1

First printing, August 1967
Second printing, October 1967
Third printing, August 1968
Fourth printing, July 1970
Fifth printing, October 1973
Sixth printing, July 1975
Seventh printing, June 1977
Eighth printing, February 1979

PHOTOLITHOPRINTED BY CUSHING - MALLOY, INC.
ANN ARBOR, MICHIGAN, UNITED STATES OF AMERICA
1979

FOREWORD

This book is dedicated to the proposition that Christian doctrine — rooted in Scripture, oriented to the Reformation heritage, and related to contemporary issues — is still of fundamental importance.

The story of this handbook goes back a short way to 1964-1966, when these thirty-two brief chapters first appeared as a series of study guides for churches and schools. In that original format they were tried and tested in various fellowship clubs, discussion groups, adult education programs, catechism classes, as well as Bible doctrine classes in high schools. Now, after some extensive editing, they are being published in this form.

Obviously no claim is made for exhaustive treatment. Rather this selection of doctrinal studies is designed to serve in the Christian community as a kind of self-starter for personal enrichment and group discussions.

The chapters follow generally the accepted order of the major headings in systematic theology, namely, the doctrines of God, man, Christ, salvation, the church, and eschatology, with an introductory section on religion and revelation. A pertinent Bible reading suggestion accompanies each chapter. Each chapter is broken down into meaningful sub-divisions. Relevant questions intended as pump-primers to stimulate a free exchange of ideas are interspersed throughout the chapters at convenient stopping-off points.

Submitting to the Bible as the primary rule for faith and practice, drawing upon some of the classic creeds of the Christian Church, and standing upon the shoulders of great Christian thinkers of past centuries, this study guide seeks to focus basic Christian doctrines upon the life of the Christian community in the world today.

CONTENTS

What Is Religion?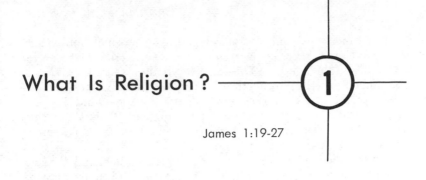

James 1:19-27

Christian doctrine is a grand house, with foundation, building blocks, girders, roof, and windows looking out. It has many doors giving entrance from the front, the back, and the sides, opening upon every room in the house. Above the main entryway to this house of Christian theology is the password: Life is religion. The "welcome" mat is out. Come on in!

Diagnosis

The question of religion is literally as old as the hills. Yet as the question behind all questions, it surrounds us at every turn as inescapably as the weather. For religion is the very atmosphere in which we live and move and have our being.

Many well-meaning people are pleading these days for putting the fourth R back into public education, alongside of the old stand-bys, Readin', 'Ritin', and 'Rithmetic. The cry goes up: They have taken away my Lord out of the schools, and I know not where they have laid him! Enact legislation to get Religion (prayer and Bible reading) back into the curriculum.

Many bewail our commercialized Yuletide and preach the gospel: Put Christ back into Christmas! Let's make it a religious holiday.

You often hear "people who think young" declare: Religion is not for me. Religion is for aged people (as a substitute for robust living) and for old fogies (who insist on playing ostrich) and for little children (who don't know better). Maybe I'll take up religion when the time comes.

Wherever you turn, it's the same story. Don't drag religion into the lecture hall. Keep religion out of politics. Labor organizations are religiously neutral. Business and religion don't mix.

Most Americans conceive of religion as a personal hobby and a private affair between a man and his God (or whatever he takes to be his god). This is everybody's sacred privilege, guaranteed by the "freedom of religion." We will respect it, even defend it, as long as you keep it personal and keep it private. No one is really opposed to religion. Polls show that 93 percent of Americans believe in God. Just so you keep it in its place, as one slice in the total pie of life. But I'll take a different slice. God, you stay in your little corner, and I'll stay in mine. Agreed? For religion is sacred, and marketing is secular, and never the twain shall meet.

We glory in our high and mighty wall of separation — a more formidable barricade than any Berlin Wall. And the First Amendment secures it. But hasn't a subtle shift taken place from separation of church and state (and rightly so) to separation of religion and public life (and wrongly so)?

1. In what sense can the United States and Canada be called Christian nations?

2. If we define secularism to mean "a life detached from God," is secular humanism the prevailing religion in America?

3. What is the basic error in all the above-mentioned (mis)conceptions of religion?

Response

Popular Christian sentiment talks religion too. You overhear it almost any day of the week: "Oh, my neighbor, why, he's got no religion at all." Or: "She's a very religious person." Or as one recent convert to another: "When did you get religion?" During the war it was proclaimed far and wide: "There are no atheists [non-religious people] in foxholes."

True enough, there are no atheists in foxholes. But nowhere else either. Of course, there are armchair atheists. And sometimes we Christians think and act very much like practical atheists when we overlook God. But actual atheism is a sham.

At bottom, atheism — pretended nonreligion, supposed detachment from God — is self-deception. Only fools say there is no God (Ps. 14:1). And "abominable works" follow this creed. Sophisticated people may spend a lifetime suppressing all semblance of religion. A renegade may mount a pulpit, clench his

fist in God's face (if there be a God), and from God's failure
to strike him down conclude that there is no God. Socialites
may eulogize the "Titanic," boasting that even God couldn't sink
this ship (if indeed there be a God).

Yet Paul would say of us as of the Athenians, "In all things I
perceive that ye are very religious" (Acts 17:22). But with a
difference: The Athenians publicly displayed their religious
loyalties, whereas we try to drive ours into a corner. Calvin gets
at the heart of the matter in saying that all men are "incurably
religious" (*Institutes*, I, 3). Religion is given with our creation.
Being human means being religious. Religion is this built-in
relationship of responsibility to God. The question is therefore
not whether a person will have a religion or not, but what the
nature of that religion will be. Hence missionaries, wherever
they go, find religion in operation. The very denial of God is
itself religion in reverse. In this world therefore the true
religion coexists with many false religions.

4. Why is professed atheism utter folly?

5. Does our experience confirm scriptural teaching that religion
   is universal?

6. What forms does practical atheism take in our lives?

Heart and Life

Paul pursues the same line of thought in Romans 1:18-23.
Sin did not destroy religion, but perverted it, turning man to
worship and serve some creature instead of the Creator. But
give allegiance to someone or something man must do and,
in fact, does.

James, the very practical theologian, distinguishes "vain religion" and "pure religion" (1:26, 27). True religion means being
"doers of the word" (v. 22). Religion is not something to be
forever debated, but lived. For religion is life, namely, "to visit
the fatherless and widows in their affliction, and to keep oneself unspotted from the world."

In the opening chapters of the *Institutes* Calvin discusses
the "seed of religion," which, manifesting itself in the "sense
of divinity," produces "piety" (a right set of the heart) and
"religion" (a right way of life).

Scripture pictures religion as rooted in the "heart," out of which are all the issues of life (Prov. 4:23). The more than eight hundred references to "heart" in the Bible point to it as the core of man's personality, the central directing force in his life. "As a man thinketh in his heart, so is he" (Prov. 23:7). Jesus said: "The good man out of the good treasure of his heart bringeth forth that which is good; and the evil man out of the evil treasure [of his heart] bringeth forth that which is evil: for out of the abundance of the heart his mouth speaketh" (Luke 6:45). The set of the heart sets the course of our religion which, in turn, sets the pace of our lives.

7. With the help of a good concordance discover in the Bible additional examples of the use of this concept "heart."

8. What implications does the centrality of the "heart" have for our thinking (intellect, e.g., education), feeling (emotions, e.g., courtship), acting (will, e.g., work and recreation)?

9. What does Paul mean in saying, "Their god is their belly" (Phil. 3:19)?

10. What are some of the gods of modern men?

11. Is James endorsing the slogan, "Not doctrine, but life"?

Covenant

If the "heart" is the religious fountainhead that waters all of life, then life as a whole is religion. That is, all of life, in all its dimensions, in its full scope, in all its interrelatedness — the whole man, in his total existence, throughout the whole world of his experience — answers to God's claim upon us. This is the covenant — God's promise, our response — everywhere, always, nothing excluded. This is religion. This is the life!

12. Are we often guilty of narrowly restricting the covenant to childbirth, infant baptism, covenant nurture, Christian education, rather than pouring into it the total content of our living?

Religion and Revelation

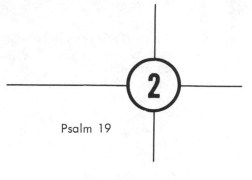

Psalm 19

The most basic question a man can ask is the question of authority. The Christian settles this question by an unwavering appeal to an authoritative revelation, which offers firm footing for his confession: "Here I stand, I cannot do otherwise; so help me, God!" With Peter and Paul, the Christian stakes his claim to truth, not on "cunningly devised fables" (II Peter 1:16), not on "science falsely so called" (I Tim. 6:20, A.V.), but upon the living Word of a revealing God. Christianity is therefore a religion of revelation. For religion is man's response to God's revelation.

Many twentieth-century thinkers have rededicated themselves to the proposition that the doctrine of revelation is, after all, still of fundamental importance. Yet there is little unity in viewpoint. In facing this central issue at the crossroads of current theological debate, we reach a parting of the ways in Catholicism, Barthianism, Fundamentalism, Calvinism, and other systems of thought.

Fact and Faith

The Reformed faith views revelation as a sovereign act of God. We cannot manipulate God or maneuver Him into a position where we can subject him to scientific analysis. We can but listen as He chooses to expose us to his ways and works in creation, history, conscience, and supremely in Christ. Our entire store of knowledge is dependent on the good pleasure of our revealing God. For nought have we gotten but what we've received. Man does not enter the world with a fund of innate ideas, which as seeds bud forth into flowering fruits by some inner drive. Rather, we are created with an implanted impulse to absorb the varied aspects of God's revelation as they enter our world of experience. True knowledge comes by discovery, not by invention.

The core idea in revelation is the notion of "unveiling." Think of unwrapping a gift, or unveiling a monument, or drawing aside the curtains at a playhouse. Revelation, accordingly, means making known something previously unknown and still unknowable apart from the revealing act of him who possesses all knowledge.

Revelation is both fact and faith, event and meaning. It thrusts us into a living encounter with God, the world, and ourselves. It is in the world, yet not of it. By deeds and words God imparts heart knowledge concerning his claim upon our lives and his plan for the world — opening doors of understanding which would otherwise remain forever closed.

A knowable God and a knowing man — this is the foundation of true religion. But God dwells in "light unapproachable." To commune with us, He must and always does speak anthropomorphically, that is, in human form. He casts his Word into human words. Even his names, personal revelations, are drawn from earthly vocabularies. See how He stoops to conquer us, lisping as a Father to his children. He gears his revelation down to our level of understanding. He limits his revelation to our capacity and our need. There are hidden depths we cannot plumb, dazzling heights we cannot ascend. Yet the light that shines is, though filtered, true. And in that light we see light (Ps. 36:9).

1. Why does Communism call religion "the opiate of the people"?

2. Explain in what sense the question of revelation and authority was the central issue in the sixteenth-century Reformation.

3. Try to arrive at some understanding of the views on revelation as held by the schools of thought mentioned in the second paragraph of this chapter.

4. What is the significance of the rending of the veil in Matthew 27:51 for our understanding of revelation.

5. What does Hebrews 1:1, 2a teach us about God's revelation?

6. Many Liberals proclaim a resurrection-faith without a resurrection-fact. What do you think about this gospel?

7. Interpret Christ's deed and word in Matthew 9:6 in the light of this emphasis on both fact and faith.

Word of God

The Bible spells out various aspects of revelation in its use of the concept, *Word of God.*

In the beginning God spoke his *creative Word,* out of nothing calling into existence heaven and earth and all things therein. His creative Word is not merely a pious wish, but an almighty and effective command. God spoke, and it stood fast (Ps. 33:9).

Progressively God spoke his *prophetic-apostolic Word.* Even before the fall God revealed to Adam the covenant and the cultural mandate. After the fall God met man in his need for redemption by gradually unveiling his plan of salvation through Moses, Samuel, and Isaiah, through Peter, John, and Paul.

In time revelation took the form of the *inscripturated Word.* Since oral revelations are transitory and subject to loss and distortion, God chose to preserve his revelation for succeeding generations by recasting it into a written record, the Scriptures of the Old and New Testament.

Today we still hear echoes of God's revelation in the *preached Word.* In its preaching and teaching ministry, the church stands in the tradition of the prophets and apostles, who held the preached Word as no less authoritative than the written Word.

Finally and decisively God gave the world his *incarnate Word.* Christ Jesus (John 1:1, 2, 14). What more can God say? He that has seen and heard Christ has seen and heard the Father.

8. Think through this fivefold Word to discover the Christocentric revelational unity running through it all. What is the significance of the fact that Christ is both the creative Word (John 1:3) and the redemptive Word (John 1:14)?

9. What authority should we attach to preaching today?

10. Can Christians get along without the written Word?

Two Books

The whole story has been published in "two books" (Belgic Confession, Article II). Not that God engages in double talk.

For there is an unbreakable bond between God's fundamental (general) revelation and his redemptive (special) revelation. The Reformed Christian must be schooled in both volumes. For a sound understanding of their complementary unity forms the only firm foundation for a Christian world-and-life view, for Christian education, and for a healthy view of our calling in the world.

The world is a mirror reflecting its Maker. Sin did not shatter the mirror. How could Satan undo God's handiwork? Rather, God's fundamental revelation, originally uni-focal (revealing the goodness of God, Gen. 1:31), became bi-focal (revealing both the goodness and the severity of God). If only we have eyes to see!

The Scriptures are spectacles to refocus our distorted eyesight. Scripture is not a substitute for general revelation, but a restorer of it. It is not a textbook in science, art, and culture, but a guidebook for all of life. It is a lamp to our feet and a light upon our path (Ps. 119:105) as we explore (education) and utilize (vocation) the manifold resources of God's world.

11. Are there conflicts between the Bible (redemptive revelation) and science (fundamental revelation)?

12. Can we worship God in nature?

13. Should Christian liberal arts colleges be converted into Bible colleges? Christian day schools into evangelistic agencies?

14. Should Christians stick to the Bible alone, since too many people lose their faith in science and art?

15. Is it true that being a minister, missionary, or evangelist is the "highest calling" in life? that only such people are "full-time kingdom workers"?

The Inspiration and Infallibility of Scripture

II Timothy 3:14-17; II Peter 1:19-21

3

Authority

Inspiration and infallibility: What content shall we pour into these articles of faith? With the Belgic Confession we affirm "that God, from a special care which He had for us and our salvation, commanded His servants, the prophets and apostles, to commit His revealed word to writing" (Art. III). . . . "against which nothing can be alleged" (Art. IV). . . . "believing without any doubt all things contained in them" (Art. V).

The Reformed Creeds are relatively silent on the doctrine of Scripture. This reflects the fact that, whatever the sixteenth-century conflicts among Catholicism, Lutheranism, Calvinism, Zwinglianism, and Anabaptism, there was general agreement on the doctrine of Scripture. Hence the confessing fathers felt no need to explore the point at great length. Biblical criticism is a typically modern problem. In facing it, we must reach back through the creeds to Scripture. For, being our highest authority, only Scripture can answer our questions about Scripture.

How, then, was it possible for God to pour a heavenly message into earthen vessels? How could the infallible Lord speak through his otherwise fallible servants without his message losing its authoritative ring and religious imperative? The answer lies in the mystery of inspiration, assuring us of an infallible rule for faith and practice.

1. Upon what does the authority of Scripture rest?

2. How do we distinguish scriptural authority from the authority claimed for, say, the Koran or the Book of Mormon?

3. Why do we relate the work of inspiration specifically to the third Person in the Trinity?

4. Why do our creeds devote relatively little attention to the doctrine of Scripture? In rewriting the creeds today, would we place the emphasis differently?

5. Is it "circular reasoning" to insist that our doctrine of Scripture be derived from Scripture itself?

Transmission

In reflecting on the Bible, we must distinguish between autographs, manuscripts, and versions. Autographs are the original writings as they came from the hands of the Bible authors. As far as we know, none are in existence today. Kuyper suggests that God provided for their disappearance to prevent men from idolizing them (cf. the brazen serpent, II Kings 18:4). But we are not left empty-handed. We have hundreds of manuscripts. Though there are some troublesome variations in textual readings, more striking is the careful preservation of the Bible down through the ages. Recent discovery of the Dead Sea Scrolls serves to confirm Christian confidence in the faithful transmission of the Bible.

Now, inspiration is a unique work of the Holy Spirit, applying specifically and exclusively to the original inscripturation of God's Word. Yet, in view of sound textual criticism and careful transmission, we may confidently embrace the Bible in our hands too as the Word of God. The Word of God did not get lost with the disappearance of the autographs.

6. Do you agree with Kuyper's view?

7. Can we speak of an inspired and infallible translation of the Bible, as is suggested by Roman Catholic attitudes toward the Latin Vulgate Bible?

8. Were the Reformers right in pressing for Bible translations in the language of the people?

9. What do you think about the great increase in the number of translations in modern times?

Authorship

The Bible has a double authorship, divine and human. In the interrelationship between the primary Author and the human authors lies the heart of the mystery of inspiration. There are three main theories which address themselves to this question of the mode of divine inspiration.

The mechanical-dictation theory eclipses the human factor, suppressing the personalities of the human writers, regarding them as passive instruments, automatons. Differences in style, grammar, vocabulary, and insight must then be ascribed to differing moods in the overriding work of the Spirit.

The dynamic theory in fact excludes the divine factor. Scripture is regarded as the product of the religious literary genius of godly men. As such it ranks with the great spiritual lore of all ages.

The organic view seeks to do justice to both the divine and human roles in inspiration, honoring the mystery by confessing the Bible to be both fully and truly divine, and fully and truly human. It emphasizes the active participation of the human authors under the sovereign superintendence of the Spirit.

Since Scripture is its own interpreter according to the analogy of truth, look at two classic passages on inspiration.

Paul in II Timothy 3:16-17 teaches that all the writings of sacred Scripture are "God-breathed." But this is not some abstract truth. For this inspiredness undergirds the Bible's profitableness in disciplining faith ("for teaching, reproof, correction, instruction in righteousness") and practice ("unto every good work"). Implied is the idea of divine authority and trustworthiness covering "all scripture," in all its varied literary forms, whether history, psalms, proverbs, prophecy, parables, symbolism, or law. But to each belongs its own method of interpretation.

Peter in II Peter 1:19-21 makes the same bold claims. Scripture came by divine initiative ("from God"). But in the process of inspiration men were swept along in its Spirit-energized thrust ("moved by the Holy Spirit"), making them active communicators of the message ("men spoke").

10. Can you illustrate the serious shortcomings of the mechanical and dynamic views?

11. How do Revelation 1:19 and 21:5 show the sovereign guidance of the Spirit in inspiration? How do Proverbs 25:2 and Luke 1:1-4 show the active participation of the human writers?

12. What parallel can you point out between the mystery of inspiration and the mystery of the two natures in Christ?

13. Do you think that Paul's words "all scripture" also include the spoken words of Jesus?

14. What practical, profitable value can we derive from the doctrine of inspiration?

Infallibility

The infallibility of Scripture is dependent upon, and defined by, its inspiration. Since inspiration is plenary (its total scope) and verbal (its full depth), it is also infallible in its whole extent and in all its parts. Scripture never corrects or criticizes itself. Though it warns against false confidence in itself, it never warns against overly enthusiastic confidence. Rather, in those matters on which it claims to speak, it speaks infallibly, in the sense of not letting us down, not misleading us, not deceiving us. Hence infallibility means trustworthiness, which also suggests what should be our proper attitude in response to the Scripture.

This truth is highlighted in Matthew 5:18 (cf. Luke 16:17), where Jesus teaches that God's Word ("the law") holds sovereign sway in history, that its message stands unchangeable ("in no wise pass away") and irreducible ("not one jot or tittle"). It is, of course, not for the words and syllables as such in their abstract isolation, but for the words and syllables in their ordered sequence, as conveyors of the message in the living flow of truth, that Jesus claims infallibility, that is, trustworthiness (worthy of our trust).

The same truth is forcefully expressed in John 10:35 ("and the scripture cannot be broken"). Jesus teaches here that even the literary forms carrying God's Word as vehicles of communication are inviolable, and therefore cannot be slighted with impunity.

We may not claim too little for Scripture. It is, for example, more than a fallible human witness to God's revelation. But we may not, on the other hand, claim too much. The Bible is not, for example, a handbook illustrating perfect grammar, or pure vocabulary, or ideal style. To distort Scripture by understatement is to impoverish it. To distort it by overstatement is speculation. And both are exceedingly hazardous (Rev. 22:18-19).

We must evaluate Scripture infallibility only by the standards which the Scripture itself endorses, consistent with its own divinely appointed intent and purpose, which is discoverable only by submissive, responsive, and diligent Bible study.

15. Show the interrelationship between inspiration and infallibility in the two passages at the head of this chapter.

16. In our everyday living how should we respond to the "trustworthiness" of Scripture?

17. What bearing does Revelation 22:18-19 have upon our understanding of the infallibility of the Bible?

18. Is it permissible to apply the statistical accuracy of a computer or the mathematical precision of the scientific method to our interpretation of scriptural infallibility?

Scripture–Our Canon for Faith and Life

Jeremiah 36:1-28

Confession

This is our confession: "We believe that the Holy Scriptures are contained in two books, namely, the Old and the New Testament, which are canonical, against which nothing can be alleged," and: "We receive all these books, and these only, as holy and canonical, for the regulation, foundation, and confirmation of our faith; believing without any doubt all things contained in them" (Belgic Confession, Articles IV, V).

The word "canon" (hence also "canonical" and "canonicity") is derived from the Greek *kanon*. Its root meaning is "reed" or "measuring rod." Secondarily it signifies "established list" or "sphere of authority." Eventually these definitions were extended to embrace the idea of "rule of beliefs" or "standard of conduct." Accordingly early Christian literature identifies the Bible as its Canon, the rule for faith and life, a concept that arises out of the New Testament itself (Gal. 6:16; Phil. 3:16)·

Biblical canonicity is an article of faith, resting upon a conviction of, and commitment to, these books as the very Word of God. This is an irreducible assumption, a basic presupposition, our point-of-departure. This is our religious axiom, which, like every axiom, is beyond rational demonstration. We can only inquire into the grounds, significance, and implications of this confession.

As Augustine said, faith seeks understanding. In earnest inquiry, however, many questions and baffling problems arise. What is the source of biblical canonicity? How did this happen historically — all-at-once or bit-by-bit? Why are precisely these books included? Why were other good books excluded? What if a lost book should be found? When were the Old and New Testament canons finalized? How can we be sure the Bible is the only true Canon? Every difficulty must, however, be handled within the framework of our faith commitment.

On peripheral matters we must often speak tentatively, remembering that to speak the final word is God's prerogative alone. But on central issues we can speak decisively. For real conflicts over the Canon were relatively few and minor, and books temporarily disputed can practically be counted on the fingers of one hand.

1. What is the meaning of the concept "rule" or "canon" in these two Pauline passages?

2. What reasons can you offer for calling one of our Forms of Unity the "Canons of Dort"? What is the relationship between the canonicity of the creeds and the canonicity of the Bible?

3. Is the Christian caught in a vicious circle in confessing: I believe in God because of the Bible and I believe in the Bible because of God?

4. Referring to the statement from Augustine, what is the relation between faith and reason?

Standard of Judgment

Luther expressed some doubts about Esther, because it lacks any direct reference to God, and he dubbed James a "strawy epistle," supposing that James weakens Paul's emphasis on justification by faith. Some scholars suggest that Calvin questioned Revelation, pointing out that he wrote commentaries on every book of the Bible except Revelation. But this is simply an argument from silence. Actually, all Calvin's writings reflect unreserved submission to the entire Canon. In this respect the Reformation churches followed Calvin more closely than Luther.

Unitedly, however, the Reformers rejected the Roman Catholic inclusion of the apocryphal books in the Canon. Through the Greek translation, the Septuagint, and the Latin translation, the Vulgate, the Apocrypha became part of the Bible. Luther, however, appealed to an early Christian distinction between canonical and apocryphal books and separated them in his German translation. The Puritans earned the name "persecutors of the Apocrypha" in removing them from the Bible. Gradually this position prevailed. Today there is general agreement on the sixty-six books among orthodox

Christians, even among Liberals for whom the distinction between canonical and apocryphal books is quite meaningless,
and partially among Catholics who identify the Apocrypha as
only deutero-canonical.

In retrospect we see three guiding principles that governed
the church in accepting the Bible as its Canon. The first criterion was *apostolicity*. The apostles were honored as the appointed transmitters of the gospel, the recognized revelatory
links between Christ and the church. To win a place in the
Canon of the New Testament, a book must be traceable to an
apostle or a close associate of an apostle.

A second criterion was *universality*. Among the countless
documents in circulation in the early church, many were short-
lived or had only a local following. But canonical status de-
pended on a book's winning universal and unanimous and permanent consent in the church.

A third criterion was *inspiration*. To win a place in the
Canon a book must breathe sound doctrine and morals, show
the time-tested marks of divine revelation, and evidence its
consistency with the rest of Scripture.

5. What is your reaction to Luther's questions?

6. What importance do you attach to the fact that the Belgic
   Confession, Article IV, gives a specific list of all the Bible
   books? Do you agree that Paul is the author of Hebrews?

7. According to the Belgic Confession, Article VI, what value
   should we attach to the Apocrypha?

8. How does Modernism drastically reduce the Canon by recognizing, say, only the Sermon on the Mount as God's Word?
   How does Revelation 22:18, 19 bear on this question?

9. How does Rome violate the Canon in the other direction by
   extending it to include tradition? How is Vatican II reviewing
   this co-relationship between Scripture and tradition?

The Canon and the Church

In retrospect we can also point out some historical factors
which influenced the formation of the Canon in the life of the
church. First, there was *Marcion's* canon, which repudiated
the whole Old Testament and reduced the New Testament to
Luke and ten epistles of Paul — all in the name of anti-
Semitism. Facing this challenge the church was compelled to

answer the inevitable question: Is Marcion right? If not, what then?

Secondly, *heretics* appealed to any available document in support of their views. Troubled by such controversy the church was compelled to define the books to which legitimate appeal could be made in support of Christian truth.

Thirdly, there was *persecution* unto death. Facing fiery trials, the church was forced to decide which books might conveniently be disavowed, and, in contrast, for which books believers should be willing to suffer.

What is the ultimate ground justifying the canonicity of Scripture?

Catholicism appeals to an *infallible ecclesiastical decree* to validate our acceptance of the Canon. Though the Bible has an inherent authority, says Rome, yet our acceptance of that authority depends on the consent of the church. But this implies a canon (namely, the church) above this Canon.

Others hold that the Spirit who inspired the Scriptures also *inspired* the church it its formulation of the Canon. But this levels out the biblical concept of inspiration, robbing it of its unique reference to the inscripturation of the Bible.

Still others appeal to a *very special providence* which, in a semi-miraculous way, governed the church in selecting its Canon. But for such transcendent illumination and supernatural intervention there is no evidence. Rather, a quite normal sifting process was at work in early Christianity.

Closer to the truth is this: The Scripture is self-justifying, because the Scripture is *self-authenticating*. By its own internal evidence and by the convincing testimony of the Spirit the Scripture won for itself an undisputed place as the decisive Canon in the believing consciousness of the church.

10. May we conclude from the three historical factors mentioned above that the Bible is just the product of historical developments?

11. Are any of these historical factors still at work today?

12. How do Rome and the Reformation differ on the relationship between the church and the Canon?

13. How does the Belgic Confession, Article V, distribute the emphasis among the three grounds for the canonicity of Scripture mentioned above?

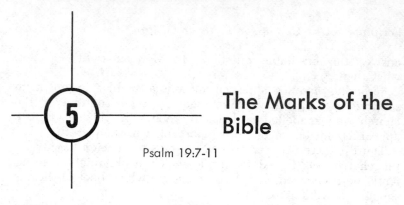

The Marks of the Bible

Psalm 19:7-11

Our doctrine of Scripture must come from Scripture itself. It is woven into the total fabric of the Bible. One of the many passages highlighting the virtues of the Word of God, viewed from the Old Testament perspective, is Psalm 19:7-11. This tribute to special revelation is a good starting point for reflection on the marks of the Bible.

Rediscovery of the Word of God, and its restoration to a place of centrality in the Christian life — this was the heart of the Reformation. Out of this revival of biblical studies in the sixteenth century came a development of the doctrine of the marks of the Bible, initially stated by the Reformers, more fully formulated by their successors. Reformation theology generally distinguishes four marks: namely, the necessity, sufficiency, clarity, and authority of Scripture.

1. What qualities of God's Word are revealed in Psalm 19?
2. Is it true to say that the Reformers rediscovered the Bible?

Necessity

For God, of course, biblical revelation was not a necessary act, but a free choice. But for us, such a fixed word revelation was necessary to preserve the Bible from loss and change. Moreover, in view of our sinful human predicament, if we are to be liberated and illumined, the Bible comes not as an added convenience, but as a dire necessity. It is the answer to our deepest need. As Calvin says, "Take away the Word, and faith will perish. It is the very source of Christian life. It is the charter of the church."

Quite understandably, therefore, the Reformers protested Rome's failure at this point. Catholicism does not, of course, teach that the Bible is wholly unnecessary. But both by precept

and practice it teaches men to regard the church as more necessary than the Bible. For the Bible owes its origin, authority,
and interpretation to the church. Rome's failure to stress the
supreme necessity of the Word reflects itself traditionally in its
overriding emphasis on ecclesiastical authority, long-standing resistance to placing the Bible in the hands of the people, and
neglect of preaching.

The Reformers were also loyal churchmen. But to them the
church is the servant of God's Word, not its lord. Therefore the
church itself must bow in confessing the supreme necessity of
Scripture.

From another quarter, mysticism came as an attempt to
eclipse the necessity of the Word in the name of a higher spiritual illumination. The letter killeth, the Spirit maketh alive,
these mystics claimed, downgrading the Word in the name of a
supposed inner Light. But how can the Spirit, who gave the
Word, make his own Word unnecessary!

3. How does the warning, "My people are destroyed for lack
   of knowledge" (Hos. 4:6), apply to our times?

4. How does John 8:31 emphasize the need for close fellowship
   with God's Word?

Sufficiency

To the Reformers the Bible is our only redemptive revelation.
But this is no weakness. For it is at the same time adequate,
unabridged, needing no other books alongside it, and wholly
sufficient unto the intent and purpose for which it was given. In
it God's plan of salvation and his will for our lives is so fully revealed that no man can say, "God is holding back on me."

Hence the Reformers' firm stand against the mystics' reliance
on ecstasy, charging the Bible with inferiority and shortcomings. What more could God say! The Bible is enough to hold
man inexcusable for his unbelief.

Hence also the Reformers' opposition to the Roman Catholic
doctrine of two sources of revelation, Scripture and tradition.
The prophets and apostles have spoken in one Book. There we
have a revelation of God's work in Christ so supremely sufficient
as to make rulers and prelates, councils and creeds subject to its
authority.

The Bible does not contain all of divine revelation. Nor does it answer every conceivable question. Nor is it a textbook in every field of human knowledge. But it is a redemptive guide-book for all, in all.

5. If the Bible is sufficient, why do we need sermons, creeds, Bible outlines, and commentaries?

6. Does the sufficiency of Scripture mean that it is an encyclopedia on every field of study?

7. What is wrong with basing one's faith on personal experience instead of on the Bible?

8. Which contemporary religions deny the sufficiency of Scripture by holding to other books besides the Bible?

Clarity

The medieval church held that the Bible was so hard to understand that it is useless and even dangerous to entrust it to common Christians. Simple minds should rely, not on their own reading, but on the instruction of the church. For the Bible is complicated, and needs an infallible interpreter.

The Reformers responded that Scripture is not dependent on synods or theologians to remove its obscurity. It is basically intelligible and meaningful to every submissive and responsive reader. No inquirer can really miss its message. Failure to grasp it is due only to the self-inflicted results of sin. The Bible reveals, does not conceal. Its revelation is indeed limited by our creatureliness and by our need, but what is given is unmistakably clear.

True, the church is a mother, leading and feeding her children. But her pedagogy is necessitated, not by Scripture's lack of clarity, but by our slowness of heart to believe.

No one, of course, denies deep mysteries, unfathomable truths, and problem passages that baffle even the best of scholars. Nor does our confession of clarity rule out the need for careful searching of the Scriptures, or qualified teachers, or an educated ministry. Moreover, we must sometimes end with tentative explanations. And always we must leave the last word to God. But still God has spoken with such clarity that no man can say, "I don't get it."

9. What does Psalm 119:105 teach about the clarity of Scripture?

10. Can anyone ever really excuse himself from Bible study by insisting that the Bible is too hard for him?

11. If the Bible is clear in its teachings, why are there so many conflicting denominations and interpretations?

Authority

Adding things up at this point, this is the conclusion: Scripture being necessary, sufficient, and clear, it stands as the Christian's supreme authority in doctrine and practice.

The Catholic fathers did not cancel scriptural authority, but compromised it by making it dependent upon the consent of the church and counterbalancing it with the authority ascribed to tradition.

Reformation thinking could tolerate no such divided allegiance. Its byword was *sola scriptura* (Scripture alone). The Word of God exercises full and final sway. Even the church stands under its judgment.

Modern liberalism undercuts the authority of Scripture by recognizing only some parts of the Bible (for example, the Sermon on the Mount) as God's Word and robbing the whole of its redemptive power. Modern dispensationalists fall into a similar trap in refusing to recognize the present authority of the Old Testament in the life of the New Testament church.

But either we give the authority which the Word claims for itself our uncompromising loyalty, or we will one day find that Word rising in judgment against us (John 12:47-48).

12. How does Scripture in John 12:47-48 and Hebrews 4:12 emphasize its own authority?

13. What are the consequences of making scriptural authority dependent upon the church?

14. Why do dispensationalists disown the authority of the Old Testament?

15. Does the decline in Old Testament preaching nowadays reflect a declining sense of respect for the authority of the Old Testament?

Our Knowledge of God

Isaiah 12; 40:25-31

Heart Knowledge

The heartbeat of the Christian faith and life is the knowledge of God, whom to know is life eternal, here and now, and forever. Knowing God, the key to Truth is ours. For in thy light we see light. The simplest believer, therefore, knowing God, is wiser than the most learned unbeliever. To really know ourselves and our world we must know God. Without this knowledge, first and foremost, all other knowledge is mistaken and deceptive.

For the fear of the Lord (a heart knowledge of God) is the beginning (the basis) of wisdom (knowing what life is really all about). The Bible pictures true knowledge in countless shapes and colors, but it all comes down to this: We grow in the knowledge of God by growing in the grace of our Lord Jesus Christ.

Christian thinkers have translated this central theme into many, many languages. Augustine put it this way: To know God and yourself is the chief thing. Thomas Aquinas leaves us these words: Theology teaches about God, is taught by God, and leads to God. John Calvin states it thus: All the wisdom we possess, which is true and sound wisdom, consists of two parts, the knowledge of God and ourselves. Such God-centered thinking and living is the foundation of a Christian home and school and church and society.

By the knowledge of God we mean not that knowledge which God possesses in himself, but the knowledge of himself which He imparts to us. In all his words and works God discloses something of his relationship to man and the world. And we are called to embrace this knowledge with all our heart and soul and mind and strength.

It is therefore more than mere head knowledge. We could conceivably memorize all the doctrines and definitions about

God without really knowing God. A candidate for the ministry could pass his classical examination on Part One of Theology with flying colors, and still lack a true knowledge of God. Christ accused the rabbis of being strangers to God, even though they were experts in doctrine. The knowledge of God runs deeper than intellectual competence.

Similarly the knowledge of God is more than mere feeling. Religion, for many people, is no more than a sentimental experience, an emotional lift. They want sermons to be inspirational, not instructive. Give us ecstatic, tear-jerking, mountaintop experiences, they say. But the knowledge of God runs deeper than emotions.

The knowledge of God is also more than mere activation of the will. Some people read the Bible as a code book of *do's* and *don't's*. Or they listen to sermons as outlines of programs, projects, and activities to carry out. But the knowledge of God runs deeper than stimulating the will.

These three views are too limited and unbalanced. For true knowledge of God is a matter of the heart, out of which are all the issues of life. It embraces the whole man, directing the intellect and emotions and will. Heart knowledge does not exclude the head, the feelings, and the hand, but rather emcompasses them all. Therefore as a man thinketh in his heart, so he responds to God and man and the world in his mind, emotions, and will.

1. What does Proverbs 4:23 mean when it says that out of the heart are the issues of life?
2. In what sense does a Christian know things differently than a non-Christian?
3. Why should preaching and teaching be not merely doctrinal, not merely ethical, and not merely inspirational? What then?

Creator and Redeemer

As the above quotation from Calvin suggests, the knowledge of God and knowledge of self are interrelated. They go hand in hand. We gain an honest insight into our own needy condition only after we have seen God in his greatness and goodness; and at the same time, we never seriously turn to seek God until we have squarely faced our own lowliness and sinfulness.

In preaching the gospel this question hits us hard. We

wonder sometimes whether we should first confront men with themselves in order to convince them of their need of a Redeemer, or whether we should first present God in his majesty and righteousness to instill in men a sense of dissatisfaction and thus to impel them to seek their salvation outside themselves in Christ Jesus. Perhaps the answer lies in this, that you can't have the one without the other.

God has spoken twice, in creation and in redemption. But creation is first. Hence God spoke first as Creator, to man as creature, by means of creation. After sin, however, as a corrective upon our distorted vision, our view of God as Creator is restored through the redeeming revelation in the Bible.

In both revelations God comes to us in Christ through the power of the Holy Spirit. For already in creation we read that "through him [Christ] all things were made . . . that have been made" (John 1:3) and that "the Spirit of God moved upon the face of the waters" (Gen. 1:2). In redemption too we read that "he that hath seen me [Christ] hath seen the Father" (John 14:9) and that the Spirit "shall guide you into all the truth" (John 16:13).

Our knowledge of God is therefore God-centered in such a way that it is also Christ-centered and Spirit-centered. It is also man-centered in such a way that the Heidelberg Catechism confronts us with this question: What does it profit *you* that *you* know all these things?

Faced now with two revelations as sources of the knowledge of God, we find that we cannot know God as Creator until we first meet him as Redeemer. Not that creation lost its revealing power or clarity. It is still forceful and clear. It is not a "broken mirror." It did change from being uni-focal (the goodness of God) to becoming bi-focal (the goodness and wrath of God). But, worst of all, our eyesight was blinded. Now, through redemptive revelation, our eyes are opened to see God in his judgment and grace at work in his world.

4. Explain how it happens that the knowledge of God and the knowledge of self are so inseparably interrelated.

5. In preaching, what answer would you give to the question raised above?

6. What do we mean by saying that the Bible is like a pair of spectacles to correct our faulty vision?

7. Why must we know God as Redeemer in order to know Him aright as Creator?

The Sovereignty of God

Central to our knowledge of God is his declaration of sovereignty. God is God. We have learned to understand many divine attributes: God's love, his power, his justice, his mercy, his wrath, and so forth. These are properties and qualities which belong uniquely to God. But behind them all is that divine prerogative which we call sovereignty. God is accordingly sovereign in his love, in his power, in his justice, in his mercy, in his wrath, and so forth. Again, He is sovereign in creation, even in the fall, also in providence and redemption and the consummation of all things. As Lord of grace and glory, He therefore awaits our acknowledgment of his sovereignty in our homes, schools, churches, recreation areas, labor unions, political parties, social-action organizations, and all down the line.

The knowledge of God is never abstract or theoretical, but always personally and concretely related to our lives. The question is not, What is the being and essence of God in himself? But, Who is God to you? It is a knowledge of God that draws us into a living encounter with him, which transforms our hearts and reforms our lives. The knowledge of God, compelling and inescapable, always draws out of us one response or another. The right response is this:

> *O wide-embracing, wondrous love!*
> *We read thee in the sky above;*
> *We read thee in the earth below,*
> *In seas that swell, and streams that flow.*
>
> *We read thee best in him who came*
> *To bear for us the cross of shame;*
> *Sent by the Father from on high,*
> *Our life to live, our death to die.*

8. Can you explain why and in what sense Christianity emphasizes the sovereignty of God?
9. Why is it important to maintain that the knowledge of God is personal and practical?
10. What is the relationship between the two song verses quoted above?

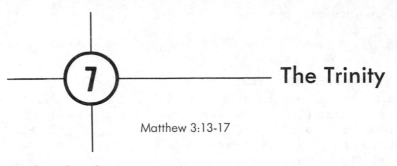

7

The Trinity

Matthew 3:13-17

In the Church

"I believe in God the Father, God the Son, and God the Holy Spirit." This is the very heartbeat of the Christian worshiping community. In our liturgies the ministers pronounce the benediction in the name of the triune God. Children are baptized "in the name of the Father and the Son and the Holy Spirit."

The Apostles' Creed itself is built up around this trinitarian theme. An ancient tradition says that the twelve apostles, before leaving Jerusalem, each contributed one article to form the Apostles' Creed. However, this creed most probably grew up gradually between the second and fifth centuries. In its earliest form it was probably a very simple statement: "I believe in God the Father and the Lord Jesus Christ and the Holy Spirit." But facing new challenges, the early church expanded its creed bit by bit to express its faith more fully. So finally it came to embrace the twelve articles as we confess them today.

The Nicene Creed is also based upon this trinitarian confession. According to the Athanasian Creed too, ". . . the catholic faith is this: that we worship one God in Trinity, and Trinity in Unity." In these creeds we can feel the fathers struggling for words to express what they held in their hearts. For we are confronted here with the heart of hearts of the Christian faith, the mystery of the Godhead. In reflecting upon it, we must begin and end in an act of adoration. And our thinking all along the way must be carried on in the same spirit of reverential worship.

1. Explain the various ways in which the trinitarian faith of the church comes to expression in our worship services.
2. Why is the Apostles' Creed called an ecumenical or catholic creed?

3. How can we make the doctrine of the trinity clear and somewhat understandable for children?

In Theology

Many Christian thinkers also used this trinitarian theme as the structurating principle in their books on Christian doctrine. Calvin, for example, divides his *Institutes of the Christian Religion* into four parts: God the Creator, Christ the Redeemer, the Spirit the Sanctifier, and the church as God's appointed teacher to lead us into a true knowledge of the triune God.

Christian theologians also rooted their commentaries in this divine tri-unity, that is, trinity: one God, revealed in three Persons. But there were sharp disputes on the propriety of using such words as "essence" and "substance" and "subsistence" and "person" in seeking to clarify this doctrine.

Calvin displays a healthy attitude toward this question in the following excerpts: "To wrangle over this clear matter is undue squeamishness and even obstinacy. Although the Latins and Greeks differ among themselves over words, they quite agree in the essential matter. Although heretics rail at such words and certain squeamish men cry out against a term fashioned by the human mind, they cannot shake our conviction that three are spoken of, each of them entirely God, yet that there is not more than one God. What wickedness, then, it is to disapprove of words that explain nothing else than what is attested and sealed by Scripture. Really, I am not such a stickler as to battle doggedly over mere words. For I have long and repeatedly experienced that all who persistently quarrel over words nurse a secret poison. However, these words are especially useful when the truth must be asserted against false accusers, who evade it by their shifts. Yet I could wish that these terms were buried, if only among all men this faith were agreed on: that Father and Son and Spirit are one God, yet the Son is not the Father, nor the Spirit the Son, but that they are differentiated by a peculiar quality" (*Institutes*, I, 13, 3-5).

4. Explain in your own words what Christian thinkers have been trying to say in the doctrine of the trinity.
5. Do you think triplet analogies (such as past-present-future, root-branch-fruit, father-mother-child, etc.) are helpful in trying to understand the doctrine of the trinity?

In Scripture

The truth of the trinity is woven into the very fiber and throughout the *total* fabric of Scripture. It is a unique teaching of the Christian religion. We look for it in vain outside the Bible. But in the Bible it is revealed so clearly, that to reject it is to reject the Bible itself. But, since it is embedded in the total teaching of God's Word, we should not rely on a few selected "proof texts" gathered at random from its pages. The doctrine of the trinity, as every other Christian doctrine, is progressively unfolded with increasing clarity across the face of the Old Testament and on into the New Testament.

The Old Testament places a strong emphasis on the *oneness* of God. Note Deuteronomy 6:4: "Hear, O Israel: Jehovah our God is one Jehovah. . . ." Such emphasis was especially important in the Hebrew world where most peoples worshiped many gods.

But the Old Testament also points to a *plurality* in the Godhead. Note Genesis 1:26: "Let us make man in our image"; and Genesis 3:22: "Man is become as one of us"; and Genesis 11:7: "Come, let us go down, and there confound their language." This plurality comes to greater clarity, hinting at the three Persons, in such passages as Psalm 33:6: "By the word [second Person] of Jehovah [first Person] were the heavens made, and all the host of them by the breath [third Person] of his mouth." There are similar breakthroughs in Isaiah 9:6, "Everlasting Father," and Isaiah 61:1, "The Spirit of the Lord Jehovah is upon me."

Scanning the entire Old Testament, we meet regular references to God the Father, frequent references to God the Son (note the many Messianic promises), and occasional references to God the Spirit (e.g., Genesis 1:2: ". . . and the Spirit of God moved upon the face of the waters").

This trinitarian revelation comes to clear focus in the New Testament, not only in specific passages, but also in the names and honors and works ascribed to the three Persons. What is still partially concealed in the Old Testament is at last fully revealed in the New Testament.

We witness the crowded presence of the triune God, and the conjunction of activity by all Three, at Jesus' baptism, where the Son is baptized, the Father speaks, and the Spirit descends in the form of a dove (Luke 3:21, 22). Another clear testimony to the trinity is contained in Christ's baptismal formula in Matthew 28:19: "baptizing them into the name of the Father and of the Son and of the Holy Spirit." Peter's sermon on Pentecost, moreover, cannot be understood apart from apostolic belief in the trinity (see Acts 2). To cite but one more part of the whole truth, listen to the apostle's salutation in I Peter 1:2: "According to the foreknowledge of God the Father, in sanctification of the Spirit, unto obedience and sprinkling of the blood of Jesus Christ: Grace to you and peace be multiplied."

6. Should we insist on "proof texts" to support our belief in the trinity?
7. Show how the New Testament more clearly reveals the doctrine of the trinity than the Old Testament.
8. Give evidence of the doctrine of the trinity from Peter's sermon in Acts 2.

In Everything

To live a God-centered life, therefore, means Father-centered living and Son-centered living and Spirit-centered living. This is our very lifeblood. This is our triple blessing.

This cornerstone of Christianity is a stumbling block to non-Christian thinkers, both Jew and Gentile, including nowadays Liberals, Unitarians, and Jehovah's Witnesses.

But Christians dare not compromise here. For in the doctrine of the trinity the way of salvation is at stake, as is evident from the consequences of Jehovah's Witnesses theology: rejecting trinitarianism, they have rejected the atoning love of God the Father in the redeeming grace of God the Son through the sanctifying power of God the Spirit. Then faith is dead, and life barren — all their misdirected zeal notwithstanding.

9. Does the fact that the trinity is a mystery give us reason not to search out the meaning of this truth?
10. Why do Jews, ever since New Testament times, reject the trinity?
11. What beliefs do Liberal Unitarians and Jehovah's Witnesses hold which lead them to deny the trinity?
12. Should we bear witness to our faith in the trinity in our public prayers?

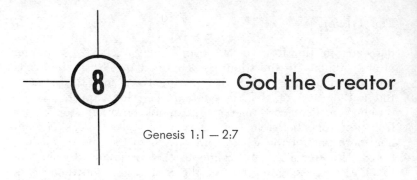

8 — God the Creator

Genesis 1:1 — 2:7

As the door to Scripture opens, immediately we stand face to face with God. "In the beginning God created. . . !" The Bible is not a book on philosophy, setting out first to prove the reality of God. There is no argument for his existence, not even an introduction. Instead, from the very start, God thrusts himself upon us as the great underlying assumption in the entire creation account. Our thinking must therefore take its point of departure in this article of faith: ". . . he that cometh to God must believe that he is . . ." (Heb. 11:6). In the beginning, God!

Genesis 1:1 serves as the prologue and title to the first two chapters of the Bible. It stresses the central theme: "God created the heavens and the earth." This, then, is the main idea, which in the following verses is developed into a booklet of seven sections, seven "days," seven acts in the drama of creation. In Genesis 1 the emphasis falls on the formation of the world, from raw materials to a finished product, with man appearing on the "sixth day" as the crown of creation. In chapter 2 God's creative acts revolve around man, appointed to serve as priest in the holy temple of God's creation. But the great presupposition is God.

1. Why don't we try first of all to prove the existence of God?
2. What duplications and differences can you see between Genesis 1 and 2? Why, do you suppose, does the Bible include these two creation accounts?

Witnesses of Creation

This grand crescendo of creative acts of God is knowable only by revelation. There are no rational proofs, no cause-and-effect chains of logic by which to reconstruct what happened. Human reason can at best offer theories and educated guesses. For, after all, who was there to witness these momentous events, except the triune God?

Hence we read in Hebrews 11:3 that "by *faith* we understand that the worlds were framed by the word of God. . . ." Therefore also with the church universal we confess: I *believe* in God the Father, Almighty, Maker of heaven and earth."

God the witness — Father and Son and Holy Spirit — at some time in history must therefore have revealed to man the basic truths about how things got started. Had God remained silent, we would be forever groping in darkness. For the three Persons of the Trinity were the only eye and ear witnesses to the birth of the world. This knowledge, revealed by God to mankind, then became a common possession of the early human race. The creation story was then passed on from generation to generation. It fanned out after the Tower of Babel episode. Finally, as oral or written tradition, it was handed down to Moses, who under divine inspiration recorded it in the Book of Genesis.

All Scripture is written in human forms and concepts (anthropomorphisms), also the creation account. The Hebrew mind of the author of Genesis is reflected in his description of the dawn of history. Genesis was written for Israel, first of all, a farming and herding community. Hence it is cast into agricultural and pastoral categories, rather than, say, into modern industrial or technological terminology. Yet, entering into this ancient mind, we discover that the language of Genesis is meaningful for believing men of all time.

The creation record is not some cool and objective theological treatise or scientific document written dispassionately by someone standing at a distance. Rather, it is the living account of an on-the-spot reporter, an observer on the scenes, standing breathlessly amid the unfolding wonders of God's hand. It is written not from the vantage point of heaven, looking down, but by someone with his feet on the ground, caught up in this action-packed drama. This is the spirit and perspective of the biblical record.

3. Why is human reason, apart from divine revelation, unable to discover the origin of the world?

4. Do you agree with the line of thought suggested above on how the divinely revealed knowledge of creation came down to Moses?

Spotlight on God

All Scripture is divine self-revelation. The creation story, too, is His-story. The emphasis falls not so much on the creation as on the Creator. We see God as the great Worker at work in the newly formed world, his workshop, with man as his co-worker. The universe is presented as a brilliant theater, with God on the stage as the leading Player in the drama of creation and with man the spectator drawn magnetically into the action. Ours is a laboring God, not the idle god of the Greeks, and Genesis offers the proper perspective for keeping the creative acts of God in clear focus.

The dynamic power behind creation was the *word* of God. "For he spake, and it was done; he commanded, and it stood fast" (Ps. 33:9). God's word is never merely a flowery description or a pious wish. It is a creative power by which God called all things into existence out of nothing by the act of an omnipotent will.

Some people have pinpointed the date of the original creation at 5 A.M. on October 26, 4004 B.C. It is doubtful, however, whether the Bible intends to give us this kind of information. "In the beginning," we read, and this is left as a dateless date. We should not look in the Bible for scientific answers to the question *when* or *how* God first put the world together. To pursue such inquiries, we must turn to general revelation. This is the province not so much of Christian exegesis as Christian geology. Here the words of Job 12:8 apply: "Speak to the earth, and it shall teach thee." Special revelation in the Word does not replace general revelation in the world, but rather illumines it. We must avoid forcing the Bible to speak on matters concerning which it is silent.

The Bible does clearly declare *who* the Originator of everything is, namely God, and *why* He did it, namely, for his greater glory and man's enjoyment. The only way to account for the world is to begin with God. Here the creationist and the evolutionist part ways. For God is the sovereign Lord of creation, or else He is neither sovereign nor God!

5. Was creation "hard work" for God?
6. What is the difference between immediate creation ("created," 1:1) and mediate creation ("made," 2:3)?
7. What role does "the Word of God" play in Scripture? (See Psalm 33:6; John 1:3, 14.)
8. When was "in the beginning"?
9. Does the Bible intend to teach us scientifically how God created the world?
10. What is the difference between creationism and evolutionism?
11. Why did God create the world?

Seven Days

The "six days" of creation highlight the orderliness and progression in God's way with the world. What about the length of these "days"? Some hold to days of twenty-four hours. There is also good reason to believe, however, that these "days" are picturesque descriptions of lengthy periods of time. In fact, many Christian scientists talk nowadays of a very old earth, perhaps millions of years old. The Bible and Christian thinking, it seems, can absorb such astronomic figures. But we must always distinguish carefully between fact and theory, for many statistics passed off in the name of fact are little more than fancy. If compelled to reject these high figures, we should do so, however, not because they are high, but because they are unfounded.

The Genesis account apparently leaves room for a dynamic concept of creation, involving process and development. Indeed, creation without process would seem to insult the wisdom of God, just as process without creation denies the reality of God.

Then "God blessed the seventh day, and hallowed it; because that in it he rested from all his work which God had created and made" (Gen. 2:3). Here, built into the original structure of things, is the divinely established pattern for our weeks of worship and work.

12. How do you interpret the biblical word "day"?
13. Do you think God used process and growth in creating the world?
14. What implications does the divine example of six days of work and a seventh day of rest have for our lives? Are we faithful in preserving this biblical heritage?

9 The Providence of God

Psalm 104

The God of creation is also the God of providence. For the Framer of the universe never deserts the works of his hands (Ps. 138:8). The work of providence picks up where the work of creation leaves off, "in the beginning," from the very first split second of history. For creation cannot exist apart from the Creator, nor can it run on its own powers. The continuation of the world, as well as its origination, is unthinkable apart from the sovereign Lord of all. Moment by moment all life — plant, animal, and man, together with all the physical forces at work in the universe — is upheld by those everlasting arms. "O Jehovah, thou preservest man and beast" (Ps. 36:6).

Alpha and Omega

Our word "providence" is traceable to the Latin word *pro-video,* meaning to look after something. As a word it is absent from the Bible. But the concept is written large on every page, if we have eyes to see and ears to hear. For only by faith can we detect the hand of God in history. Divine providence is, accordingly, not a piece of logic to be mastered, but a belief to be embraced. The starting point is all-important. If we look at life without first looking to God, we can come up with almost any answer — or no answer at all. Apart from the personal confession, "My times are in thy hand" (Ps. 31:15), and the sweeping confession, "The earth is Jehovah's, and the fulness thereof" (Ps. 24:1), men observe providence in action, but call it fate or chance or luck or destiny or the law of averages.

The inner workings of divine providence come to sharp focus in the experience of Joseph — to his father the favorite, to his brothers the dreamer, but to God the preserver and provider of his people. See there the overruling providence of God, intercepting the hostile intentions of men, bending evil unto good. But hindsight is usually better than foresight. Thus, looking back, the victim-become-victor puts his whole life story in perspective in these words, "Ye meant evil against me; but God meant it for good" (Gen. 50:20).

"I am God," says Scripture, "declaring the end from the beginning" (Isa. 46:10). The "beginning" of all things — the affairs of men and nations, the movements of planets and atoms — lies in the decrees of God. Predestination, we call it. The "end" of all things is the working out of these decrees in real life. This we call providence.

Predestination is the divine plan, knowable to God alone. Providence is the divinely directed course of life, which to us seems often disorderly and unpatterned, by which however God realizes his purposes here and now. God, as it were, thinks forward from predestined ideas to providential acts. In response, it is ours from a creaturely distance and in childlike trust to think God's thoughts after him, leaving the secret things to the Lord, and living instead by the revealed Word (Deut. 29:29), concluding from God's providential acts to "Thy will be done."

> *I sought the Lord, and* AFTERWARD *I knew,*
> *He moved my soul to seek Him, seeking me.*

Calvin discusses predestination and providence in one breath (*Institutes*, I, 16). For they are really but counter-sides of the same coin. To God there are therefore no miscues, no accidents, though to us things do apparently happen "by chance" (Luke 10:31). But actually things are in good Hands, and they never really get out of hand. On our part this does not call for a fatalistic submission to an inexorable Will, but for spontaneous concurrence and ungrudging participation in God's way for our lives.

1. What is the relationship between God's work of creation and his work of providence?
2. Is God responsible for the evil intentions and acts of men, or does He absorb them into his plan as He "treasures up his bright designs and works his sovereign will"?
3. In what sense are we called to be co-workers in the working out of God's providential plan?
4. Is it always easy and pleasant for us to accept God's providential leading in our lives?

Cosmos — Not Chaos

The biblical concept of providence expresses two main ideas, namely, that God *upholds* and *guides* all things. He is not the god of the Deists or the Secularists, a kind of absentee landlord who allows the world to run its course by "natural law." God is the Sustainer of worlds that be, ceaselessly undergirding the life and replenishing the resources of his creation. Should He withdraw, this cosmos would erupt into a chaos.

But God not only keeps things going, He also keeps things moving toward their established goals. He directs, governs, guides. Therefore, though to us his ways are often past finding out, still life does have an underlying rhyme and reason. The times are not out of joint. Things do not really go astray. For all things work together for good unto the coming of his kingdom, here and now, and in the end, until Christ is all in all.

Christian faith therefore rejects "chance" as the answer to life's questions. Things do not just "happen to happen" the way they happen. We are not senseless victims of arbitrary and capricious forces working upon us. There are laws and structures built into the world-order, which operate under the steadying hand of their Maker and Keeper, who neither slumbers nor sleeps (Ps. 121:4, 5). This confidence assures us of the regularity of life's processes and the outcome of our endeavors.

Again, "fate" is not the key to knowledge. We are not helpless pawns on some chessboard, moved about and sacrificed by the ironclad determinism of some inflexible, heartless mover. Rather, our Provider is our Father, who deals with us as children, not as mere numbers or commodities. He is indeed immutable, but not immobile, for He is moved by our prayers (James 5:16).

5. How should a Christian take to heart Paul's words, "In nothing be anxious" (Phil. 4:6)?

6. Is it harder to believe in providence nowadays than in former times?

7. May Christians make plans for the future?

8. What do you think of this attitude: If it is going to happen, it is going to happen, and there is nothing you can do about it?

Questions

Since God's ways are higher than ours, we are often left with baffling questions, which keep coming back to haunt us. Questions such as these:

1. If God's sovereign will governs everything, how can we maintain a meaningful place for free and responsible human acts?

2. If God works all things according to his immutable decrees, how is it possible for God to "change his mind" (Gen. 6:6; I Sam. 15:11; Jonah 3:10)?

3. If God overrules the evil as well as the good, how can we avoid the conclusion that God is the author of sin?

Many false notions of providence are in the air these days. Hosts of our fellows hold to a humanistic view of God as the gentle and congenial philanthropist nudging man along in his evolutionary climb toward Utopia. The doctrine of providence was further distorted by Hitler when he appealed to "Providence" (*Schicksal*) to guarantee his destiny as leader of the super-race. Others pay lip service to some vague notion of Providence as a convenient substitute for God. And now, in these post-war years, in a world groaning under the almost unbearable weight of nuclear stockpiles and gas chambers and Berlin Walls and social revolution, the spirit of nihilism cries aloud: "God is dead! Nothing makes sense! Who will show us any good?"

To men caught in their self-made world without windows and cells, without exits, the old answer of the Heidelberger may need a new language, but it still stands: "The almighty and everywhere present power of God, whereby, as it were by His hand, He still upholds heaven, earth, and all creatures, and so governs them that herbs and grass, rain and drought, fruitful and barren years, food and drink, health and sickness, riches and poverty, yea, all things, come not by chance but by His Fatherly hand."

9. How should the church proclaim the message of divine providence for our times?

10. After a narrow escape we often exclaim, "That was providential!" Is this a right response?

11. If a person rejects the providence of God, in what other ways can he explain the experiences of his life and the happenings in the world?

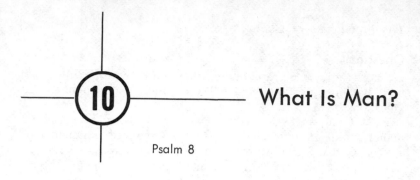

What Is Man?

Psalm 8

Stranger

Modern man's knottiest problem (as he sees it) is himself. He feels overwhelmed by a desperate sense of loneliness, even in the face of a massive population explosion. Living is existing, and life an unsolvable riddle — a sprawling jig-saw puzzle, all mixed up, with most of the pieces missing, and those that are there just not fitting! Sometimes frantically, sometimes despondently, he searches for self-identity: Who am I anyway? What in the world am I doing here? Estranged from God, man becomes a stranger to himself, and in reaction (in our times) turns himself inside out by psychoanalysis in his distraught attempts to regain his lost identity.

This is part of the absurd and senseless spirit of the mid-twentieth century. Since around the turn of the century a spiritual revolution has taken place before our very eyes. Back then men were accustomed to viewing the world through rose-colored glasses. Man, convinced of his dignity and inherent goodness, talked confidently about a perfection just around the corner. "We're on the way! Give us a little time and a fair chance, and we'll create utopia here and now. Let God retire. Glory to man in the highest!"

If the old optimism bred a deification of man, the present pessimism is leading many to dehumanize man. And both are terribly wrong. For God is God, and man is man, nothing more and nothing less. Our questions and problems may shift, but there is through it all a stable answer, which, though differently slanted, is always basically the same.

1. How is it possible for modern man to feel lonely, even in a crowd?

46

2. In what sense is the answer of the gospel to the needs of men in the mid-twentieth century different from the same answer applied to the needs of men at the turn of the century?

Servant

To be honest with ourselves, we must look into the mirror of Scripture. There we meet God. But there we also face ourselves. For, as Calvin clearly teaches in his *Institutes* (I, 1, 1), knowledge of God and knowledge of self go hand in hand. They stand or fall together. The old optimists, creating God in the image of man, were guilty of pride and pretense. The contemporary pessimists, some lamenting and others celebrating God's demise, abandon themselves to "open-ended living."

In trouble we often urge our fellows, "Get hold of yourself." But we cannot really get hold of ourselves until we lay hold on God. Augustine put it well, "To know God and myself, this is the chief thing." At the heart of this double knowledge is the confession of God as sovereign Lord, Creator and Redeemer, and ourselves his servants, made by his glory and remade by his grace. From beginning to end, therefore, the virtue that graces man's life best is humility.

Pride, on the contrary, is a symptom of distorted knowledge of both God and self.

3. In what sense does true knowledge of self go hand in hand with true knowledge of God?
4. Why is humility the chief virtue? Does this exclude boldness? Does it mean we should be everybody's "doormat"?

Creature

In the unfolding drama of creation, man appears climactically on the stage of primitive history as the crown-prince of all creation. At the peak of the crescendo of creative acts, behold Adam! That is, "man." The head of the human race appears on the scene only after the world of earth and heaven, land and sea, plants and animals are in a state of readiness to accommodate his style of living. Last, but not least! Just as a house becomes a home after people move in, so the world comes to its own only after man is ushered in.

And how? We all have a common name, "Adam," for we were created in the image and likeness of God (Gen. 5:1, 2). All creation bears the imprint of God's mind, but only man is his image. A singular honor! What privilege! What responsibility! The writer of Psalm 8 takes the words right out of our mouths.

But what precisely is this divine image we bear? To define it defies understanding, and words fail us. The image of God in man points, however, in this direction: we at a creaturely level are uniquely children of our heavenly Maker. Our Catechism describes this image as "true knowledge of God, righteousness, and holiness." In line with this definition, most Christian thinkers associate this image primarily with the spiritual side of man's existence. Yet it remains true that the whole man, in his total life, body and soul, intellect and emotions and will, male and female alike, in work and play — our whole selfhood reflects our Maker's praise as nothing else in all creation does.

> *What is man that he should be*
> *Loved and visited by Thee,*
> *Raised to an exalted height,*
> *Crowned with honor in Thy sight!*
> *How great Thy name!*

5. What does it mean that man was given dominion over all creation (Gen. 1:26; Ps. 8:6)?

6. How would you define the image of God in man? What happened to it as a result of sin?

7. The biblical idea of holding office implies God-given authority, responsibility to God, and service in creation for men. How should this kind of belief shape our lives?

Office-bearer

Facing a finished creation, with man at its helm, God exclaimed, "It is very good!" (Gen. 1:31). Not only was the world made for man, but man for the world. We may therefore never fall into a world-withdrawing spirit. For creation, even in its fallen state, now being redeemed by Christ, is still our Father's world. And He has entrusted it to us.

In the original order of things, there was no room for segregation from God, or from our fellow men, or from the world. By reason of his privileged status and rich gifts, man was appointed as the liturgical spokesman of all creation in worshiping its Maker. God the great Worker also commissioned man to be his understudy and co-worker, cultivating the earth, naming the animals, populating this globe — which, translated into modern parlance, means agriculture and industry, science and art, technology and research, music and literature, homemaking and schoolwork, and a hundred and one other tasks. This is our cultural mandate. Out of the God-directed impulses of our heart, we are called to shape a culture within us and around us (in home, church, school, society, and so forth) that will glorify him who equipped and appointed us unto this high calling.

To fulfill this God-given vocation, man was invested in the triple office of prophet, priest, and king. As prophets, it is our duty to explore the truth wherever we find it, to address it effectively to the needs of our day, and to apply it meaningfully in every walk of life. As priests, our heart being in the right place, we are called in love to demonstrate by deeds of charity the greater love of our Creator and Redeemer, serving not only as the conscience of the community, but also as the intercessors of society. As kings, it is our solemn obligation so to rule our lives and the world around us that others, beholding our good works, may glorify our Father in heaven.

8. How would you define your personal cultural mandate within the framework of your particular life calling?

9. In what ways does our prophetic-priestly-kingly office function in your life?

Behold the Man

It is true, as often stated, that comparisons are odious. Yet, comparing what God made of us with what we have made of ourselves, the conclusion is clear: our present sinful state is odious indeed. The good in us is of God; the evil, of ourselves. Hating our destructive inclinations, God yet so loved his indestructible work of creation in us that He sent into this fallen world the Man of God to reconcile his rebellious creatures. This Man, Christ Jesus, became like unto us in all things (sin excluded) to redeem our lives, to redirect us in the pursuit of our cultural mandate, and to restore us to our true prophetic, priestly, and kingly office.

Jesus Christ represents God's greatest act of condemnation upon mankind, but at the same time his greatest compliment. In God's sight the cross reflects our unworthiness, but not our worthlessness. See the price God was willing to pay to recover his original investment in man and man's world! Now, by faith, we are his workmanship, created through Christ (John 1:3) and recreated in Christ unto good works, which God beforehand prepared that we should walk in them (Eph. 2:10).

10. Was Christ truly human in the sense that He identified himself completely with us?

11. How does Christ's redemption reflect the value which God still placed upon fallen man as his greatest handiwork?

Angels and Demons

Hebrews 1; Revelation 12:7-17

Luther's Inkwell

Angels and demons? What an unearthly subject! Out of this world! After all, who still takes angels and demons seriously? This is perhaps a nice topic for idle conversation and theological speculation. But who really reckons with such outlandish creatures nowadays? The Bible does, but do we? Mr. Christian, when did you last pray God for the helping hand of one of these "ministering spirits" (Heb. 1:14)? In praying, "Lead us not into temptation, but deliver us from evil," do we ever really think in terms of a mob of demons out to get us? As the servant of Elisha, often in times of crisis we fail to see that "they that are with us are more than they that are with them" (II Kings 6:16).

Luther, you recall, hurled his inkwell at the devil. Medievalists were inclined to speculate about how many angels could dance on the head of a pin. We smile at all this, quite understandably. Yet these Christians at least took the spiritual world seriously. True to Scripture they recognized, though with blurred vision, that there is a world beyond this world; that there is more to life than just persons, places, and things; that experience is richer than mere touching, tasting, and seeing; that the spiritual world is as real as the physical. We moderns, absorbed so totally in our physical and mathematical sciences, are tempted to fall for a "you are what you eat" philosophy of materialism, counting body more important than soul, and accordingly angels less real than dollar bills, and demons more farfetched than germ warfare. But to adopt this frame of mind is to put oneself out of touch with reality, to lose sight of one of life's deepest dimensions.

Many thinkers today argue that the Bible offers no basis for a serious discussion of angelology and demonology. The Bible does not open up a world-and-life-view touching on heaven and earth, angels and demons, it is argued. For it speaks only of man in relation to God. Indeed, the Bible is addressed to earth and its inhabitants (men), not to heaven and its inhabitants (angels), nor to hell and its inhabitants (demons). Therefore many of our questions regarding angels and demons are left unanswered. Yet, in casting its light upon the God-man-world relàtionships, the Bible, at almost every crucial turning point in the history of redemption, in all but three or four of its books, introduces us to angels and demons as real and important personages. Hence Christian faith is prompted to inquire into the nature and task of angels, both the upright and the fallen.

In this area of truth, as in all others, there is a progressive unfolding in the clarity and fullness of scriptural revelation. Generally speaking, the Old Testament picture of angelic and demonic forces remains quite vague and indistinct until the prophets of the exile. In Ezekiel, Zechariah, and especially in Daniel, the picture comes into much sharper focus. In the New Testament, at last, especially in events surrounding the life of Christ, we begin to see and feel quite unmistakably the full impact of angelic and demonic activity.

1. Do we really take angels and demons seriously in our every-day living? Should we?

2. Can you offer evidence to show that the Bible reckons realistically with angels and demons?

3. What do you think about Luther's impulsive act?

Legions on Command

Even college students sometimes evidence a tendency to think of spiritual realities (angels and souls) as in some sense divine. In Scripture, however, these all are creatures of God, belonging to the finite and temporal order of things.

Yet angels possess a kind of superhuman wisdom and power, enlisted as messengers of God in the service of men. They are called "sons of God" (Job 38:7), that is, echoes and agents of God's will. The divine title, "Lord God of *Hosts*" (e.g., Luther's hymn, "Lord *Sabaoth* his name"), points to God as the Commander-in-Chief of these heavenly legions (Matt. 26:53) who are ever able and willing to answer the call of divine duty. In the Lord's Prayer we are taught to look up to the angels as our examples in obedience: "Thy will be done on earth as it is in heaven," that is, "grant that . . . every one may discharge the duties of his office and calling as willingly and faithfully as the angels in heaven" (Heidelberg Catechism, 124).

What is the point of Psalm 8:5: Are men superior or inferior to angels? This is probably a wrong question to ask. We are crowned with a glory and honor that is denied the angels, and vice versa. Men and angels belong to such different orders of creation that real comparison is impossible. To each his own — this is the rule — and all under God.

Among these legions there are the rank and file angels, but also those clothed with greater authority. In the Old Testament the Angel of the Lord appears at significant junctures in history (e.g., Josh. 5:13-15). Michael is the archangel (Jude 9), the special guardian angel of Israel (Dan. 12:1). Gabriel is the heavenly herald (Luke 1). The cherubim (quite in contrast to common sentimental notions about "cherubs") are the sturdy watchmen surrounding the throne (Ezek. 10). The seraphim are the confessors and worshipers in heaven's courts (Isa. 6).

The history of redemption is punctuated regularly by angelic interventions. They were joyful witnesses of creation (Job 38:7), agents in giving the Mosaic law (Gal. 3:19), announcers of the Messiah's birth (Luke 2:13), sustainers of Christ in his temptation (Matt. 4:11) and in his suffering (Luke 22:43), interpreters of the ascension (Acts 1:10, 11), rescuers of apostles (Acts 12:7-10), and they will be divine assistants in the final judgment (Matt. 13:41; 25:31) — to mention only a few of the hundreds of biblical references.

But are angels still active today? Many Christians have relied heavily on belief in guardian angels. Each Christian, it is argued, especially each Christian child, enjoys the protection of his personal guardian angel. This case is still wide open. But Christ does say of children that "in heaven their angels do always behold the face of my Father who is in heaven" (Matt. 18:10). The Bible gives no warrant, however, for shifting trust in God to trust in angels, for the latter are, under God, providential agents in the service of believers.

4. Does the Bible give us any idea concerning when the angels were created?
5. Describe as fully as you can the task of angels.
6. What do you think about the question of guardian angels?

Demonic Forces

In the background of man's fall looms large the fall of the angels. Who, and when, and how, and why? We cannot tell. But this insurrection (II Peter 2:4; Jude 6) unleashed fearful demonic forces in the world. The nineteenth century, drunken with its evolutionary optimism, closed its eyes to evil around us. This century, more realistic, speaks of demonic powers at work in contemporary lawlessness, in atomic holocausts, in the satanic spirit of the concentration camp. These "adversaries" are formidable! We deceive ourselves if we write them off easily. But the kingdom is coming, for, as Christ said, "If I by the finger of God cast out demons, then is the kingdom of God come upon you" (Luke 11:20).

The chief villain is Satan, head of these diabolical henchmen, alias "Beelzebub" (Matt. 10:25), "prince of this world" (John 14:30), "the great dragon" and "the old serpent" (Rev. 12:9), "a roaring lion" (I Peter 5:8), "an angel of light" (II Cor. 11: 14).

Blasphemy assumed its most hellish proportions when Christ himself was accused of being in league with Beelzebub (Matt. 12:24) and of being possessed of demons (John 7:20; 10:20). One cannot fall lower than the bottomless pit. Yet Satan is a diehard, fighting a losing battle, but never giving up. He has been "judged" (John 16:11), and his doom is sealed. Yet very religiously ("the demons also believe, and shudder," James 2:19), he and his host push their lost cause. Nevertheless, Luther is right:

> *And though this world, with devils filled,*
> *Should threaten to undo us,*
> *We will not fear, for God has willed*
> *His truth to triumph through us.*
> *The prince of darkness grim,*
> *We tremble not for him;*
> *His rage we can endure,*
> *For lo! his doom is sure,*
> *One little Word shall fell him.*

7. Does the Bible shed any light on the above questions of who, when, how, and why the angels fell?

8. What is the relationship, as you see it, between demonic activities and the catastrophes of our times?

9. What does Job 1:6-12; 2:1-6 teach us about the relationship between God and Satan?

10. In what sense is Christ the Victor over demonic powers?

11. What can we learn about demonic temptations from the book by C. S. Lewis, **Screwtape Letters**?

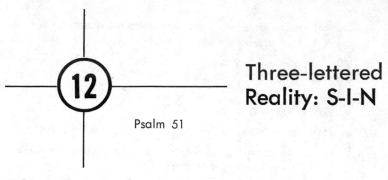

Three-lettered Reality: S-I-N

Psalm 51

Taking Sin Seriously

History has it that President Calvin Coolidge, reputedly a man of few words, upon returning from church was asked by his wife, "What did the minister preach about?" To which the President replied, "Sin." "Well, what did he say about it?" the First Lady countered. The answer came, "He was against it."

Seriously, however, I suppose "being against it" is, after all, about the most significant attitude one can assume toward sin. For obviously God is very much against it, and the Bible and our confessions and liturgical forms too.

Yet how can we face up to sin realistically and take a resolute stand against it in a world (though we are not *of* it we are nevertheless *in* it) where sin is either bypassed or reduced to a psychological guilt complex or environmental conditioning or a regrettable consequence? Such redefinition dulls our sense of responsibility toward sin and its effects in us and around us. Modern psychology has indeed helped us plumb some of the mysterious depths of the human personality, but left us with the knotty problem of the relation between sin and sickness. Modern sociology has helped us understand how a bad environment contributes to delinquency, but has also left the impression that the slum (rather than the human heart) is the root of sin. And we all know only too well that it is easier to show remorse over the results of our sins than to be sincerely repentant over sin itself.

Nowadays, however, we see a noticeable "advance" over the goody-goody theology of the previous century. Mid-twentieth century man is seized by a sense of frustration in the face of evil forces running wild in our world. Men go berserk and shoot up the works. Everyone assumes graft in politics. Our world lives from crisis to crisis. High school dropouts pose an alarming problem. Our streets are not safe after dark anymore. Most men, they say, are two-timing mates. The "new morality" is capturing our campuses. Dope is as common as aspirin. Korea today, according to reliable sources, is a veritable cesspool of sexual iniquity, engulfing 90 percent of our servicemen. And the atrocities of the last war!

At the Eichmann trial in 1961, three British journalists commented as follows (remember, these were not Calvinist preachers expounding on total depravity, but hard-nosed reporters discussing world events): "No human being is perfectible" (take note, all liberal prattlers about the inherent goodness of man)! Continuing, "Man has an infinite capacity for evil"; "There is a little Eichmann in us all"; and "That little Eichmann becomes a big Eichmann in times of crisis."

Our newspapers offer eloquent testimony to the sins of society, the sordid and seamy stories, the perverted and derelict characters, among both the underprivileged and the elite. Remember Profumo, Billy Sol Estes, Bobby Baker? And what about the news that never rates the papers!

Our world is giving sin a "new look." How shall we view these things? We must once again, as Christians, adjust our spectacles (the Word of God) to set our sights clearly on self and sin and society.

1. What can psychology and sociology teach us about man's sinful nature?

2. How do you explain the fact that we are often more concerned about the evil consequences of our sins than about our sins themselves as offenses against God?

3. Do you think that men today are more open to serious discussion about sin and evil in society and in their personal lives than men around the turn of the century?

4. Is man's sinful nature coming to more explosive expression nowadays than in former times? Are men worse than ever today?

An Honest Book

Today's literature is unblushingly honest. Nothing, neither the innermost secrets of the heart, nor life's most intimate relationships — nothing escapes its searching and searing literary analysis.

But the Bible is an exceedingly honest book too. Indeed, more honest — honest-to-God and honest-to-life. For it not only shuts us all up under sin, but also provides an exit to newness of life. As a mirror, the Bible shows us up for what we really are. As a two-edged sword, it cuts through our sham, our makeup, our veneer of decency, our overlays of pretense. It is a searcher of hearts. Honestly, without fear or favor, it judges the sins of the ungodly, but no less the sins of the saints — Adam, Noah, Abraham, Moses, Samson, Eli, David, Hezekiah, John, Peter, and Paul who calls himself the chief of sinners (I Tim. 1:15).

How did things get to be this way? The answer lies in Genesis 3: "In Adam's fall we sinned all," putting it in the words of the New England Primer (cf. Rom. 5:12-21). This is the sin behind all sins. Yet this was but the second act in the drama of sin. The first act takes us back to the fall of the angels (see previous chapter), which is the background to man's fall.

He who sows the wind must reap the whirlwind. What a harvest of iniquity among men! Original sin, with its aftermath of guilt and pollution: sickness and sorrow and death and hell. Actual sins of word and thought and deed. And we dragged the whole world down with us. Now even "all creation groaneth and travaileth in pain" (Rom. 8:22). O sin, what hast thou done to God's fair world!

Sin, sinfulness, sins, sinners: what a mess! Did we then by our rebellion dethrone God? This is unthinkable. God is sovereign even over sin. He so ruled and overruled sin, and still so governs and controls it, intercepting and using it, that in Christ his grace subdues our sin. Confess God's dominion over sin as strongly as you will, but always short of making him the author or cause of sin. For causality implies responsibility, and responsibility for sin stands diametrically opposed to the whole biblical teaching about God.

5. In what sense is the Bible more honest than the realistic literature of our times?

6. Illustrate, with examples from the lives of the men mentioned

above, the honesty of the Bible in showing that even the holiest of the saints has but a small beginning of perfect obedience.

7. How are we all involved in Adam's fall? Refer to Paul's teaching in Romans 5:12-21. Is there a parallel between our involvement in Adam's sin and our involvement in Christ's redemption?

8. In your own words describe the biblical relationship between God's sovereignty and man's sin. Did God cause it? will it? permit it? or what?

Biography of a Sinner

Sin thrust an antithesis into life. It put man at odds with God, and at odds with himself, his fellows, and his world. Turning on his heels, man ran away from God, reversing the direction of his life. He was not reduced to a beast. He did not lose his humanity. He remains human, but religiously out-of-joint, turned topsy-turvy. He lost the image of God, not in the sense of being shorn of some faculties, but retaining everything he had before, finding them all out of kilter. This is total depravity, living on an anti-godly frequency. All this is bad indeed, but it could be worse. For demons are absolutely depraved, that is, beyond the realm of redemption. We, as believing men, can always say, "Thanks be to God, who giveth us the victory through our Lord Jesus Christ" (I Cor. 15:57).

But the victory begins with an open confession of our personal and corporate bankruptcy. We will have to swallow our pride, and nod approval as the Bible writes our biography, the biography of a sinner, through the pen of David in Psalm 51.

What are the charges against us? These: wickedness, corruption, depravity, disobedience, unfaithfulness, apostasy, iniquity, unrighteousness, to mention but a few! Me? Am *I* really that bad? The Catechism picks up the case: "incapable of any good and inclined to all evil." But surely that is laying it on a little thick! There is no escape, however. The Bible has the goods on us: "The heart is deceitful above all things" (Jer. 17:9). It puts *our* words in Paul's mouth: "Wretched man that I am!" (Rom. 7:24). "All we like sheep have gone astray" (Isa. 53:6). For "There is no distinction; for all have sinned, and fall short of the glory of God" (Rom. 3:22, 23).

Apart from God's intervention, we would still be blazing

our blind trails, and stumbling aimlessly down our labyrinthian ways, and running stuck in our dead-end streets. But somehow, somewhere, God met us on our Damascus Road and set us straight.

9. What does it mean that we are totally depraved?

10. In what sense is David's autobiography in Psalm 51 also our life story?

11. How do you account for our readiness to nod approval when the preacher talks about our **sin** and sinful nature in general, but object strongly when he hits our personal **sins**?

Common Grace ⎯⎯⎯⎯⎯⎯ (13)⎯

Psalm 145

Splendid Vices

The doctrine of common grace is not commonplace in Reformed circles. It remains one of our knottiest problems, especially when it comes to a Christian evaluation of non-Christian culture and its products. To handle it aright requires a large dose of sanctified common sense and an uncommonly large measure of special grace.

Already back in the sixteenth century, Calvin in his *Institutes* (II, 2, 12-17) led the way in wrestling with this complex question, when in almost a single breath he called non-Christian science and art "good gifts of God" and at the same time "splendid vices." This paradoxical judgment points up the enormities of the problem and the crucial place it occupies in Christian thought and life. For the common grace question is rooted in the central biblical message of sin and grace.

On the one hand, what is not born of faith is sin (Rom. 14:23). Hence the world of unbelief rests under the awful vengeance of God. And rightly so, for in our fallen world no man doeth good, no not one (Rom. 3:12). Therefore God is angry with the wicked every day (Psalm 7:11). Yet behold the goodness as well as the severity of God. For He is kind even toward the unthankful and evil (Luke 6:35).

Sin is the biblical background to grace. For in grace God counteracts our sin by judging it and pardoning it in Christ. Here then is the real antithesis in the world: grace and wrath, forgiveness and condemnation, belief and unbelief. As Christians, renewed and redirected in heart and life, we are what we are by the undeserved and forfeited favor of our Creator-Redeemer. But does the grace and goodness and longsuffering of God also overflow to the unbelieving, unregenerate world?

The Bible leads us to an affirmative answer: The whole world of nature and men is still our Father's world. All creation lives by the grace of God.

1. How would you harmonize the two expressions above as quoted from John Calvin?
2. What is the Biblical teaching on the relation between sin and grace?
3. What kind of false antitheses do we often set up in our lives? For example, body versus soul, heaven versus earth, realm of nature versus realm of grace, science versus the Bible, Sunday versus the weekday.
4. Do you believe that God in some sense expresses a favorable attitude toward unregenerate men?
5. Should we distinguish between sin and the sinner?

The Great Divider

Whatever favor God bestows upon his fallen creature is rooted in Jesus Christ alone. For apart from him the world lies captive under the curse of sin, which we have brought upon ourselves. This grace of our Lord Jesus Christ is anchored once for all in the cross.

The cross stands in the world as the great unifier, reconciling God and man. But the cross is also the great divider among men. The very day of the crucifixion separated the scoffer and the penitent. And ever since, confronting the cross, men have fallen into two camps, two cities, two kingdoms. Yet on both sides of the great divide, Christ is Lord of all. As cosmic Lord He is also King of common grace. Thus God maintains his sovereign claim upon all men, all institutions, all cultures, however rebellious and apostate.

God's grace, working redeemingly in the lives of the elect, also works restrainingly in the lives of the unregenerate. By grace, through faith, we are given a new life principle and a new way of life. Still, quite imperfectly, for we are ever plagued with divided allegiances. The line of the antithesis cuts right down through our hearts. The good that I would I do not, and the evil that I would not, that I do! (Rom. 7:19). Oftentimes, therefore, we too need the restraining hand of God's common grace to check sin in us, until finally his redeeming grace shall have fully triumphed.

If, since the fall, man is incapable of any good and inclined to all evil, how can we account for the fact that life is still livable, that this is not a veritable hell on earth, that things are not always or ever as utterly bad as bad can be, and that many despisers of God and his Word often render decent and commendable and useful services to the community at large? There are at least three possible answers. First, one can tone down total depravity, regarding man as only partially depraved, and therefore also still partially good. Or one can deny that the unregenerate man can in any way do anything which in any sense can be called good. A better answer is faithfully to acknowledge man's total depravity, but account for his life practice being better than his religious condition by recognizing the temperings of God's common grace.

A countless crowd of people walk in darkness across the stage of history — Plato, Aristotle, Cyrus, Caesar Augustus, Cicero, Kant, Hitler, Khrushchev, the lady around the corner, the unbeliever next door, the enlightened pagan at the next lathe. We are not strangers to their problems, for we are sinners too. But we are more — saved sinners! This is God's redeeming grace to us, undeserving men. But is He unconcerned about the others? Has He abandoned them unreservedly? No, only in hell is divine wrath unmixed with patience.

6. In what sense is the cross both the great unifier and the great divider among men?

7. Are common grace and special grace two kinds of grace in God's dealings with men, or is it better to say that the one grace of God works redeemingly in some and restrainingly in others?

8. How do we experience the antithesis in our lives?

9. Do we as believers participate in common grace too, or do we live exclusively by special-redeeming grace? Give examples.

10. Do you think life would be unbearable apart from common grace?

11. Analyze the three answers given above to the question at hand, and indicate which answer you consider best and why.

12. Do you think it possible that the tribulation of the last days may result from the increasing withdrawal of God's common grace restraints upon men's lives?

The Giver's Gifts

In this life God showers blessings without number upon all his creatures. Yet only faith sees the Giver in the gifts. Still God continuously upholds the laws and structures of his universe as a whole. All men alike breathe the same air and work in the same world. We face the same facts. We share many of the same benefits. This is God's undifferentiated favor, common grace blessings, given not for the sake of the individual, but for the creation as a whole. There is therefore still some sanity in society. Not all men flagrantly violate God's creation ordinances — for example, to be faithful in marriage and honest in work. By all kinds of temporal means God bridles man's rebellious nature.

Restraining grace is not, however, a halfway house to redeeming grace. Nor does common grace provide a "common ground" between believers and unbelievers. For common grace does not wipe out the antithesis but only makes possible a measure of peaceful, though often uneasy, co-existence in a divided world. For the set of a man's heart is all-important: As a man thinketh in his heart, so is he (Prov. 23:7). It makes a world of difference whether a man's heart is in the right place or not. Our religious starting point charts the direction of our lives. For we will never really discover truth at the end of our syllogisms if we fail to confess the Truth at the outset and then lead all our thoughts captive to the Truth (II Cor. 10:5).

Still, there is no man from whom we cannot learn. For by his common grace God maintains the laws and structures of the universe both in the human mind and in the world out there. That is why unbelievers too can and do arrive at correct statements of fact, though their total religious-philosophical framework discolors everything that goes into it. The unbeliever operates with stolen goods, holding in his hands the real goods, but perverting them. He is basically mistaken, having taken God's truth, but taken it amiss.

All this has far-reaching implications for all life, especially for Christian education and Christian social action. It has to do with being in the world, but not of it. On the one hand, it keeps us from world-withdrawal and wholesale rejection of everything non-Christian, from sectarian haughtiness and aloofness. On the other hand, it warns the "church" against easy accommodation and uncritical acceptance of the "world." Some Christians claim: "I am a common grace man!" Others assert: "I am for the antithesis!" This is a false dilemma. We must maintain a biblical balance between the two. But in it all the central accent must fall on the *admiratio Dei* (admiration of God), as Calvin puts it, the adoration of God for what He is still able to accomplish in and through his fallen world.

13. Why is common grace not a halfway house to special grace?

14. Does common grace lay a common ground on which believers and unbelievers stand without difference?

15. What are the implications of the doctrine of common grace for Christian education? For Christian social action in labor and politics?

16. Why is it wrong to choose either for common grace or for the antithesis?

17. How do you explain the fact that some communities are more orderly and law-abiding than others? Is government a divine instrument of common grace?

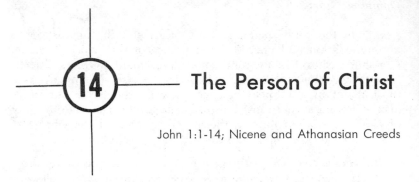

The Person of Christ

John 1:1-14; Nicene and Athanasian Creeds

Scriptural Witness

It is time now to remove the sandals from our feet, for the place whereon we stand is holy ground. In coming to Christ we enter the inner sanctum of the "mystery of godliness."

"I believe . . . in Jesus Christ, His only begotten Son, our Lord; Who was conceived by the Holy Spirit, born of the virgin Mary." What shall we say of these things? Facing this unspeakable Gift we must begin and end in an act of adoration, and all our careful thinking in between must similarly breathe a spirit of worshipful reverence.

We endorse this article of the Christian faith. We confess the truth of the incarnation. We bow before the mystery of salvation. We lead our thoughts captive to the Man of God. But by what authority? Our guide must be Scripture alone, nothing more and nothing less.

See the image of the person of Christ as it emerges from the pages of the Word. He confronts us, on the one hand, as the Son of David, the Child of Mary, the Man of Sorrows. He has all the marks of true and full humanity. He was hungry, tired, tearful — like us, whose place He came to take. He lived our life from the womb to the tomb. He grew in wisdom and in stature. He too had to learn obedience. He was acquainted with trials and temptations. In all points He was like unto us, except for sin.

On the other hand, He is at the same time Immanuel, God with us. All the glory, majesty, and power of heaven are forever his, by divine right, though for a time He laid aside his matchless sovereignty for our sake and for our salvation. In him dwelleth the fullness of the Godhead bodily. In all points, therefore, He was also unlike us, for He is very God of very God. This is the consistent witness of the prophets, looking ahead, and the apostles, looking back.

This witness is true to the claims of Christ himself. He openly acknowledged his earthly human ties with family, nation, mankind, and disciples. Alluding to his physical frame He could say, "This is my body." Reflecting on his servant's role He confesses, "The Father is greater than I." Still, at the same time, his claim stands, "I and the Father are one," and, "Before Abraham was I am," and "Father, glorify thou me with the glory which I had with thee before the world was." The whole biblical record stands or falls with these personal claims.

These claims, however, allow for no double personality in Christ. There is no divorce between his human and divine natures. There He stands, the one Christ of God. He is the Lord of glory, yet his blood was trampled under foot at Calvary. All this, without schizophrenic contradiction and without a Dr. Jekyll and Mr. Hyde kind of double life. Compellingly He calls us to confess the reality of both natures within the unity of the one Person.

What shall we do with these claims? We can regard it all as a fantastic pretense on his part, a sham, thus making Christ a deceiver and a liar. Or we can hold that Christ actually took himself seriously as a divine-human Personality, though contrary to fact, and thus expose him as a religious crank or a psychopathic victim of his own wild imaginations. Or we can argue that his passionately dedicated and overly zealous followers remade the historical Jesus into the divine Christ. In any of these cases, He is not worthy of our trust. Or we can accept his claims at their face value. The Scripture leaves no doubt as to the right alternative.

1. Why is reverence for this mystery of such great importance in seeking to understand who Christ is?

2. Do you think the Christian creeds and the doctrine of Christian theologians are true to Scripture as our guide to understanding the doctrine of the person of Christ?

3. What does it mean that Christ is wholly like us in all things (sin excluded) and at the same time wholly unlike us in all things?

4. Is there any evidence in the Bible for a personality clash in the life of Christ?

5. How would you react to the various arguments concerning Christ's claims as briefly stated above?

Ecumenical Councils

In the crosscurrents of controversy the early church faced the decisive question, "What think ye of the Christ?" The Christological struggles between liberalism and orthodoxy in the nineteenth and twentieth centuries are, under new faces, but replays of the Christological conflicts of the fourth and fifth centuries.

The Council of Nicea in A.D. 325 brought the prolonged trinitarian controversy to rest with a clear confession of the *deity* of Christ. Arius had argued that Christ was divine, but of a lower order than the Father. Athanasius (whose views shaped the Athanasian Creed) arose as the defender of orthodoxy. Belief in the full and true deity of Christ prevailed at Nicea. For a time, however, it seemed that Athanasius had won the battle, but lost the war.

In A.D. 381 the church was forced to face the question of the real *humanity* of Christ. Apollinaris, a staunch admirer of Athanasius, in reflecting on the question, *How* did God become man? in his zeal for the deity of Christ trimmed down his humanity. The church rightly sensed that our redemption is as much at stake in maintaining the humanity as the deity of Christ. The Council of Constantinople therefore reaffirmed the full and true humanity of our Lord.

The question then arose concerning the *relationship* between the two natures in Christ. The decisive and lasting importance of the Council of Chalcedon in A.D. 451 lies in its classic confession on this point of Christian faith. The churchman, Eutychus, argued from the *unity* of the Person to the unity of the natures in Christ, concluding that the divine and human merged into a third kind of intermingled being. Nestorius, on the other hand, argued from the *duality* of the natures to a duality of persons in Christ, wedging his way toward a split personality. The fathers of Chalcedon, reaffirming Nicea and Constantinople, sought to safeguard the Mystery by declaring that the two natures coexist in Christ without confusion (vs.

Eutychus), without change (vs. Arius), without division (vs. Appolinaris), and without separation (vs. Nestorius). Thus Chalcedon charted the future course of Christian thinking, the heresies to be averted, the truths to be confessed, and the Mystery to be honored.

6. How does the question of the person of Christ constantly come up in present-day controversies between liberalism and orthodoxy?

7. Can you give an explanation of other modern denials of the deity of Christ (for example, Unitarians, Jehovah's Witnesses, and so forth)?

8. What can we learn for Christian faith today from the story of the early Christian councils as sketched above?

Names of Christ

What's in a name? In ours, not much. But in the Bible, names are often revelations of the person: Moses, Samuel, John the Baptist, Peter. Yet men sometimes fail to live up to their names, as in the case of Judas, meaning *God be praised.* Of Christ, however, we rightly sing, "He is just the same as his lovely name." His names are legion in Scripture. Let's take a few, as suggested by the letters of the early Christian password, *Ichthus,* spelling *fish* in Greek, but meaning *Jesus Christ, God's Son, Savior.*

"Thou shalt call his name Jesus," announced the angel, "for He shall save his people from their sins." This was his personal, given name. It was not a new name. It grew out of the Old Testament name Joshua, meaning *Jehovah saves.* It was a common name: in a town the size of Nazareth there were probably twenty boys bearing that name. Behold the depths of the Incarnation, Christ's great humiliation and condescension, his identification of himself with the mankind He came to redeem. He became like unto us in all things, his name included.

Christ, meaning *Anointed,* based on the Old Testament name *Messiah,* was our Lord's official name. The seeds of the Old Testament flower in the New. Also rooted in the Old Testament, in the Book of Daniel, is Christ's most common self-designation, *Son of Man.* He uses it frequently in connection with his passion ("The Son of Man must go up to Jerusalem") and his second coming ("Ye shall see the Son of Man returning upon the clouds of heaven").

Christ's most exalted name is *Son of God*, relating him to the eternal order of things. At the baptismal christening ceremony, hear the Father speak: "This is my beloved Son. . . ." Down through the ages this name has been a stumbling block to unbelievers, a rock of strength to Christians.

Last but not least, Paul especially has taught us to call him *Lord.* This name embraces two main ideas. Christ's lordship bespeaks his rightful *ownership* of us, his redeemed possession. As King his claim covers every square inch of the universe. Second, as Lord all *authority* is his in heaven and on earth. His Word is therefore our command, since we are his subjects and servants.

9. Offer as much biblical evidence as you can to show that biblical names were intended to reveal something about persons and places.

10. How many names of Christ can you glean from the Bible?

11. What does the Heidelberg Catechism, Lord's Days 11, 12, and 13, teach us about the meaning of Christ's names?

Christ—Prophet, Priest, King

I Peter 2:1-10

Context

Calvin sets in sharp focus the biblical teaching that there is no participation in the *work* of Christ without participation in the *person* of Christ. We derive no benefits from the *work* of Christ without union with the *person* of Christ. We cannot possess what Christ *did* for us without also embracing what He *is* for us. These two truths go hand in hand. They are unbreakable links in the chain of redemption, bound together inseparably by the biblical idea of the *office* of Christ. The previous chapter concerned Christ as the divine-human *Person*. This chapter treats His three-fold *office*, and the following chapter will discuss Christ's redemptive *work*.

As Christians today, seeking a better understanding of our faith, we are deeply indebted to the many fathers of our faith. Among them due credit must go to Calvin as the first Christian thinker to work out systematically the biblical doctrine of the offices of Christ. "In order that faith may find a firm basis for salvation in Christ, and thus rest in him," says Calvin, "this principle must be laid down: the office enjoined upon Christ by the Father consists of three parts. For he was given to be prophet, king, and priest" (*Institutes,* II, 15, 1). Through Christ, our triple Office-Holder, God bridged the otherwise unbridgeable gulf between sinful man and a righteous God. We being fallen prophets, priests, and kings, God provided this Prophet, Priest, and King to serve as our Substitute in the plan of salvation.

The Heidelberg Catechism captures the genius of Reformation faith on this point in Lord's Day 12: "Christ is ordained of God the Father, and anointed with the Holy Spirit, to be our chief Prophet and Teacher, who has fully revealed to us the secret counsel and will of God concerning our salvation; and our only High Priest, who by the one sacrifice of his body has redeemed us, and makes continual intercession for us with the Father; and our eternal King, who governs us by his Word and Spirit, and defends and preserves us in the salvation obtained for us."

1. Can you explain more fully the biblical doctrine of **office** as the bridging idea between Christ's **person** and his **work**?
2. What can we learn from the biblical practice of anointing a man to office as prophet, priest, or king?
3. Can you offer an answer to the question why the doctrine of the offices of Christ had to wait until the sixteenth century to be seriously developed?
4. Explain as fully as you can the three main points contained in the Catechism answer, Lord's Day 12, above.

Old Testament

All of Bible history clusters around this theme, the threefold office. In the beginning man was created as prophet, priest, and king to live in the world under God. As prophet man knew and spoke and lived the truth. As priest he responded emotionally in love to God and fellowmen. As king man was appointed to be God's vice-regent in ruling the world and exploiting its potentials.

The fall into sin did not destroy our office. Man in sin is still a triple office-holder. But no longer a true prophet, man is now a false prophet, bearing false instead of true witness. Ceasing to be a good priest, man is now a bad priest, responding emotionally to God and fellowmen in hate rather than love. As king, man continues to exercise dominion over the earth, and even regions beyond, but in the spirit of self-exaltation rather than in service to his Maker.

But God, great in mercy, rather than impeach us, or defrock us because of malfunction in office, renewed us in our offices. For Christ became like unto us in all things, assuming our nature, our triple office included. By his grace we are once again true prophets, priests, and kings, at present in principle, one day in perfection.

Throughout the Old Testament we see these three offices in operation, both as the general office of all believers and as special offices in the theocracy. The division of labors among the offices become increasingly clearer. But in the earlier stages these offices are sometimes held in combination. Aaron, for example, was priest, but Moses served as both prophet and king and at times even as priest. Samuel too serves in a triple capacity, as prophetic spokesman for God, as sacrificing priest for the people, and as kingly judge in the land.

With the establishment of the kingdom under David, however, the lines become sharper. David is king, Nathan is prophet, Zadok is priest. The seriousness of violating this divinely established order is evident from the attempts of Saul and Uzziah to use their kingly powers to usurp the rights of the priests (I Sam. 13:8-15; II Chron. 26:16-20).

5. Explain the great significance of man's cultural mandate (Gen. 1:28-30) in relationship to our threefold office.
6. Why did Christ assume our three offices?
7. How does the above Old Testament division of labors according to the three offices point to a divinely established "sphere sovereignty"?

New Testament

Returning to Palestine after the Babylonian captivity, Judah became a "religious" community headed by a priest. Later the kingly and priestly offices were fused and conferred upon the Maccabees. This is background to Christ's trial before Annas and Caiaphas, high priests, a thing unheard of in the Old Testament.

In the early church, too, the lines become progressively clearer. At first the apostles, besides preaching and ruling, also engaged in the ministry of mercy. Even the early deacons, Stephen and Philip, besides their priestly services, also served prophetically as evangelists. But gradually these special offices in the church, founded upon the universal office of all believers, fall into a clearer pattern, the prophetic office concentrated in the minister of the Word, the priestly office in the deacons, and the kingly office in the elders.

In the medieval church, office was withheld from the laity, being centered exclusively in the clergy. In recovering the biblical doctrine of office, the Reformers emphasized three points: 1) that as office-bearers we have received a delegated authority from our sovereign Lord; 2) that for the exercise of our office we are answerable to God; 3) that we must use our office in the service of our fellowmen. Roman Catholicism today is rediscovering something of these truths in the spirit of the Vatican Council with its new emphasis on the lay apostolate.

The office we hold as Christians stands in the light of Christ's threefold office.

Christ is our chief Prophet. He came into the world as the Word incarnate. In the temple at the age of twelve He spoke prophetically to the professors and to his parents: "Knew ye not that I must be about my Father's business?" He spoke not as other rabbis, but as one possessing authority. For his message He claims a heavenly origin. Though modernism parades Jesus as the masterful Teacher, He is more than one who tells the truth, for He is the Truth.

Christ is our only High Priest. His priestly work is prefigured in the Old Testament passover, and remembered in the New Testament sacrament. He is Priest and Lamb in one. His priestly work does not end, however, with his sacrifice on the cross. He follows this up continuously with his priestly intercessions before the throne of grace. The once-for-all character of Christ's priestly work disallows the alleged repetitions of this sacrifice in the Roman Catholic mass. Modernism empties this sacrifice of its atoning content by reducing it to a moral example for us to follow.

Christ is also our eternal King — King in his humility, King also in his exaltation. Having endured the cross, He received the crown. Now all power is his in heaven and on earth. He is King of grace and King of glory, in the church and in the world.

"Our Father in heaven. . . . Thy kingdom come. . . ." It has come, it is coming, it will come!

8. What is the relationship between the threefold universal office of all believers and the three special offices in the church?

9. What basic differences of viewpoint do you recognize between Rome and the Reformers on the question of Christian offices?

10. Give additional evidence from the New Testament to illustrate Christ's prophetic office.

11. What is wrong with the modernist approach to the prophetic office of Christ?

12. Is there any difference between Christ's kingship in the church and his kingship over the world?

The Work of Christ ──────⬤16├──

Philippians 2:5-11

Humiliation

The drama of redemption reaches its crowded climax on Good Friday and Easter. A motley array of characters moves across the stage. They all play their roles. Each player makes his entrances and his exits. There are Judas, Caiaphas, Herod, the soldiers, Pilate, John, Mary, Nicodemus, to mention no more. But Christ is still central. In him all these people live and move and have their being.

In our times it has been popular in some circles to paint a picture of the smiling Christ. The healthy, robust, laughing Hero! Yet, strangely, perhaps not so strangely, the Bible puts no smiles and laughter on his face. Oh, yes, He probably smiled at times, for He was like unto us in all things. You can almost imagine him laughing up his sleeve as the Pharisees squirm under his biting criticism. Yet the undercurrent and overtone of his life was ceaseless suffering and unbearable torments. He was the Man of Sorrows, acquainted deeply with grief (Isa. 53:3).

> Smile and the world smiles with you,
> Weep and you weep alone.

Christ felt the sting of these words. We see him in Scripture, not as a Man with a winsome smile, but as a Man of tears, one from whom men hide their faces (Isa. 53:3). Alone He walked the road of redemption, all alone, agonizingly alone, sovereignly alone.

Step by step Christ trod the descending stairway deeper and deeper into the awful state of humiliation: "Conceived by the Holy Spirit, born of the virgin Mary; suffered under Pontius

Pilate, was crucified, dead, and buried; He descended into hell." From the cradle to the grave, it was one ceaseless cycle of sufferings. This is the way it had to be, and this is the way Christ wanted it to be. For He came to give his life a ransom for many (Matt. 20:28). Was He not the suffering Servant of Jehovah (Isa. 53)?

As a twelve-year-old in the temple He had already shouldered the burden of his Father's business. Far cry from a carefree boyhood! An artist tried to capture this truth on canvas, painting the boy Jesus in Joseph's carpenter shop, lifting a beam whose shadow falls across the wall in the shape of a cross. He was the Head of the home in Nazareth, even while submitting himself to the law of parental authority which He came to fulfill and redeem. Imagine: Jesus learning obedience from a man of whom it could not be said, "Father knows best." Yet this was his Father's will, for us men, and for our salvation.

From the very start the redemptive plot thickens without relief. Launching his public ministry, Jesus was baptized in the muddy Jordan, symbolizing his submersion into the filth-laden stream of human iniquity. There followed the buffetings of Satan, the attempted assassination by his townspeople, the disappointing infidelity of his disciples, the misgivings of his family, the hostility of both church and state, the betrayal of Judas, the denials of Peter, the injustice of Pilate, the revilings of Roman soldiers, the burden of the cross, the bloody hill, but worst of all the bitter cry, "My God, my God, why hast thou forsaken me?" (Matt. 27:46).

Behold the greatest "Sinner" that ever walked the face of the earth! For God laid on him the iniquity of us all (Isa. 53:6). The physical pain must have been indescribably intense. But the spiritual sufferings even worse. For Christ carried the total weight of our transgressions. The hammer blows of God's righteous wrath rained upon him, beating him down, until groveling in the dust, his sweat fell as blood to the ground.

Here is history's only Sufferer, for all our suffering is painless next to his. The only cross-bearer, for our crosses are but shadows of his. For Christ there was no mercy, only justice, so that for us there could be grace abounding. No one could lighten his load, not Peter, nor the angel, nor Simon of Cyrene. Even his divine nature didn't ease the burden. Rather, it so undergirded his human nature that Christ did not collapse under these unbearable pressures, thus making possible an infinite sacrifice. For every ounce of strength received, another ounce of affliction was added, until the full wages of sin were paid to the last penny.

What shall we say to these things? Pity will not do. Christ wants our trust and devotion, nothing more, nothing less.

1. In what sense is Christ central in the drama of redemption?

2. Why does the Bible never present Christ as smiling? Can you nevertheless think of incidents in Christ's life that have a humorous touch to them? Is there humor in the Bible?

3. Can you offer any reasons why Mary and Pilate are the only persons named in the Apostles' Creed?

4. Did Jesus have a "normal" boyhood?

5. When did Christ's sufferings begin?

6. Why did Christ have to suffer completely alone?

Hell

War is hell on earth, we say. Yet what do *we* know about hell! This belongs to Christ, for "He descended into hell." This article of faith is beclouded by conflicting views. It was apparently one of the latest additions to the creed, dating from about A.D. 400, a time when typically Roman Catholic ideas about the intermediate state were emerging in the early church. Early Christians, as also many Roman Catholic and Lutheran thinkers today, interpreted this phrase literally. Some referred it to Christ's captivity in the kingdom of death. Others saw in it a triumphant march through hell by Christ to proclaim his victory.

The Reformers, however, were unable to find a biblical basis for these views. Therefore they were compelled to choose between dropping this article and reinterpreting it. Their sense of historical unity with the church forbade the former. Therefore, relating it to Christ's whole life, but especially to the cry of dereliction, they expressed its meaning in these words: "My Lord Jesus Christ by his hellish agony has de-

livered me from the anguish and torment of hell" (Heidelberg
Catechism 44).

7. Do you think the Apostles' Creed is misleading in placing the
   article on descent into hell at the very end of the series on
   Christ's sufferings?

8. What do you think about the decision that the Reformers made
   on the interpretation of this article?

Exaltation

Mission accomplished! Christ had stooped to conquer. So
now the cross makes way for the crown. There is a kind of
cause and effect link between humiliation and exaltation in the
life of Christ. For the joy that was set before him, He endured
the cross (Heb. 12:2). Unless the seed is buried, it bears no
fruit (John 12:24). There is a divine *must* underlying this
redemptive "success story" that accounts for Christ's graduation
from shame to glory, as He himself expounded it to the way-
farers of Emmaus (Luke 24:26).

Christ's mastery over sin and death and hell was gloriously
demonstrated that first Easter. When the resurrection dawn
broke like thunder in the garden, God set his seal of approval
upon the finished work of his Son. He arose for our justification. His resurrection is the sure pledge of ours.

The apostles then, just as disciples today, were slow to believe
the reality of it all. But Christ shattered their unbelief by his
living presence among them. He aroused in them a new hope.
What was the secret? It was partly the empty tomb, but it
was mostly their confrontation with the living Lord. Their
doubts were dispelled. Now they had a story to tell to the
nations. In their message lies the ground of our faith.

After forty impressive days, Christ ascended. The great
separation? No, for they had his abiding presence (Matt.
28:20). For Christ it meant the heavenly homecoming. For
the church it meant entering upon the "greater works" prom-
ised by the Master (John 14:12). For, leaving them, He re-
turned to them in the outpouring and indwelling of the Holy
Spirit.

Now, enthroned in glory, the reins of the universe securely
in his hands, He bestows upon us the blessings of his cross,

daily lavishes our lives with countless bounties, intercedes for us. Who said that He had retired? Unemployed? As Head of his body and King of kings He is pushing forward the program of his coming kingdom.

But one chapter remains unwritten, the grand finale. D-day is here. V-day awaits us. We live between the kingdom-come and the kingdom-to-come. The new age is upon us. The signs of the times, as neon lights, are flashing all around us. Perhaps the greatest sign of all is our very blindness to the signs. But His-story marches on. Some day these asphalt streets will turn to gold. Then, when the last curtain falls, Christ will at last be perfectly all in all.

In view of all this, how shall we now live? A little sign in a storewindow put it rightly: Live every day as though Christ had died yesterday, arisen this morning, and were returning tomorrow.

9. Explain the biblical relationship between humiliation and exaltation in the life, death, and resurrection of Christ.

10. How do you account for the divine "must" in the work of Christ?

11. What is the biblical relationship between Christ's resurrection and ours?

12. Illustrate from the New Testament that Christ's death and resurrection was the central theme of apostolic preaching.

13. Comment on the distinction often made between the resurrection-fact and a resurrection-faith.

14. In what sense can we perform "greater works" than Christ?

15. What is the work of Christ at present in heaven?

16. Do you think we give rightful emphasis to the biblical teachings concerning Christ's return?

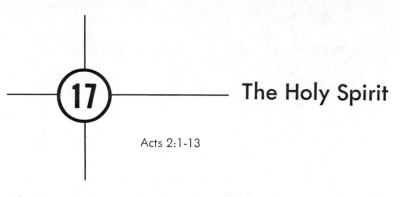

The Holy Spirit

Acts 2:1-13

The Spirit of Our Times

Every Sunday the Christian community around the world joins the church of all ages in confessing, "I believe in the Holy Spirit." Judging by our lack of concreteness in communicating this truth, however, it would appear that this witness to our faith often remains hanging nebulously, mysteriously, in a kind of doctrinal vacuum. We are often at a loss to pour real content into these verbal forms. Only on Pentecost do we explore this confession seriously, as though it were some disjointed, isolated aspect of our faith.

Meanwhile we accuse some contemporary spiritualistic movements of an almost obsessed interest in the Holy Spirit. Indeed, many evangelicals do seem to eclipse the full counsel of God by their passionate emphasis on a second baptism by the Holy Spirit. By way of reaction, modern liberalism, with its cool intellectualism, has contributed to such religious emotionalism, which thrives on ecstatic experiences, speaking in tongues, and faith healing, all of which are defended with an appeal to the igniting power of the Spirit. Noting, therefore, the rapid rise of spiritualistic sects, it is understandable that this century has been called the Age of the Spirit.

In meeting these challenges we often get off on the wrong foot. With an air of theological superiority we reply that, while the Pentecostals are narrowly Spirit-centered, and the fundamentalists are onesidedly Christ-centered, we Calvinists hold a more balanced view, for we are God-centered. Such talk may not only betray a streak of theological pride, but may also reflect the fact that we have fallen for a false dilemma. For to be rightly God-centered is to be also Christ-centered and Spirit-centered, for there is no God but the heavenly Father who comes to us in Christ the Son through the indwelling power of the Holy Spirit.

1. Do you think that present-day Pentecostalism places an unbalanced emphasis on the activity of the Spirit?
2. How has modern liberalism indirectly fostered an undisciplined spiritualism in modern sects?
3. Why are some Christians inclined to speak of the Holy Spirit as "It"?

Always on the Move

Following the history of revelation as it unfolds progressively across the pages of the Old and New Testaments, we note that the biblical accent falls initially on the Father, then increasingly and climactically on the Son, and then at the Fiftieth Day and thereafter on the energizing, transforming work of the Spirit. So we customarily speak of God the Father and our creation, God the Son and our redemption, and God the Spirit and our sanctification. Scripture leads us to honor this division of labors.

Still in all the works of God, even within this pattern of divine specialization, there is harmonious cooperation among the Persons of the Godhead and a unity of effort in every activity from the beginning. The Holy Spirit did not wait unemployed until Pentecost. From the dawn of history He was active as the life-giving Principle of all creation. The Father called the universe into existence (Gen. 1:1). The Son served as the Mediator of all created reality (John 1:3). The Spirit did not stand idly by: He moved to and fro through the structures of creation (Gen. 1:2), setting things in order and putting on the finishing touches (Ps. 33:6; Job 26:13), making man a living creature (Gen. 2:7), and continually recreating the joys of childbirth (Job 33:4). He is the inescapable Presence of every nook and cranny of human life (Ps. 139:7). For He is the very Breath of God, the ever moving Wind, which finally blew so powerfully on Pentecost. He is the Christian's native air.

Just as Christ, fully revealed in the fullness of time, manifested his concealed presence in the Old Testament, so the Holy Spirit, awaiting with bated breath the day when Pentecost would fully come, quietly went his way during the age of concealment (Ps. 51:12; 143:10; Isa. 61:1-2; 63:11; Acts 7:51).

4. How do you conceive of the relationship between the work of the Holy Spirit before and after Pentecost?

5. In asking for sanctifying grace, should we address our prayers especially to the Holy Spirit?

The Spirit of Jesus Christ

Fulfilling the ancient prophecy (Isa. 11:2), Christ carried out his redemptive mission infused with the Holy Spirit without measure (John 3:34), from the cradle to the grave. Even before the cradle, for He was conceived by the Holy Spirit (Luke 1:35). And even beyond the grave, for He arose in the power of the Spirit (Rom. 1:4). So perfect in unity is the work of the Second and Third Persons of the Trinity that Paul writes, "Now the Lord is the Spirit" (II Cor. 3:17).

Through the outgoing work of the Spirit we are brought into living fellowship with Christ. To be "in the Spirit" is to be "in Christ," no more, no less. But how is it possible to be united with Christ, living as we do two thousand years later and a half a world away? The Answer (capital A) is the Spirit (capital S). He links us to Christ, and thus binds us together. He is the living bond in the Body of Christ, the sinews, the tendons, the nerves, the muscles, making the members of the Body willing servants of their glorified Head.

This is the way Christ intended it to be (John 14:16, 17; 16:7, 13). Not through some out-of-this-world, mountaintop experience on cloud nine, but in the common affairs of everyday living. Yet so often we break the bond and thus grieve the Spirit (Isa. 63:10; Eph. 4:30).

6. Do we, too, possess the Spirit "without measure"?

7. Are there some elite Christians who by "living in the Spirit" stand above the rest of the Christian community who live (only!) "in Christ"?

8. In what ways do we grieve the Holy Spirit?

Community Spirit

Pentecost was not a one-day affair. It was for always. It made Christianity not only universal, but also forever contemporary. The Father is busy through the Son re-creating in this world a new community, whose calling it is by the illuminating power of the Spirit to try the spirits of our day. In shaping the life of the Christian community the Spirit has at his disposal four ways of working:

THE WRITTEN WORD OF GOD (Joel 2:28-32; Acts 2:16-21). The same Spirit who infallibly guided the writing of the Word now effectively drives it home to the hearts of men. Hence, from the start, biblical doctrine played an important role in the Christian church. A mark of the disciples was that they persevered in the teaching of the apostles.

THE ESTABLISHED OFFICES OF THE CHURCH (Acts 1:15-26; 6:1-6). The early church recognized the unique and unrepeatable leadership of the apostles and the regular leadership of elders and deacons for strengthening the community.

THE SACRAMENTS AS MEANS OF GRACE. Both baptism (Acts 2:38) and the Lord's Supper were faithfully administered as marks of entrance into the Christian community and growth in citizenship.

THE COMMUNION OF THE SAINTS. The cohesive power of the Spirit drew men together into a fellowship based on principle and expressed in practice (Acts 2:42). This sense of unity was born of the conviction that they all lived by one faith, one baptism, one bread and wine, one Lord, one Spirit. Now it is twenty centuries later, and that one Body is torn asunder into a thousand hardly recognizable parts!

9. Explain how Pentecost made Christianity both universal and ever contemporary.

10. In what ways is the Word of God dependent on the work of the Holy Spirit?

11. Does the Holy Spirit work differently today through the threefold office in the church than He did through the special office of apostle?

12. Do you think the countless divisions within the Christian church are a source of grief to the Holy Spirit?

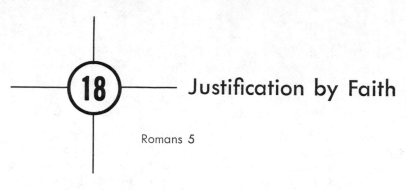

Justification by Faith

Romans 5

Do-it-yourself Religion

Caught up in the current "do-it-yourself" craze, with countless "do-it-yourself" stores, kits, and projects, we run the risk of turning religion too into a "do-it-yourself" affair. But this is nothing new. Misconceived attempts to "work out your own salvation" mark the basic trouble spot in man's religion from the beginning. Without exception, such false religious zeal ends either in deceitful complacency for those who take it easy or in frantic despair for those who take it seriously.

Whatever the merit of "do-it-yourselfism" as a hobby, when converted into a religious principle for living the good life, it falls under the radical judgment of the Scriptures. For Scripture teaches with unmistakable clarity that we are to seek our salvation outside ourselves in Jesus Christ. The biblical answer to all self-centered and self-generated religion lies in the doctrine of justification by grace alone, through faith.

> *Not the labors of my hands*
> *Can fulfill Thy law's demands.*
>
> *Not what my hands have done*
> *Can save my guilty soul;*
> *Not what my toiling flesh has borne*
> *Can make my spirit whole.*

Yet the history of mankind is a record of repeated futile attempts to win our way to glory. With sickening regularity Israel relied upon its sacrifices, its feasts, its tithes to justify its being at ease in Zion. The Pharisees' meticulous program of works-righteousness called forth Christ's scathing denunciations. In the early church Paul was moved to stress the gospel of justification by faith alone against a paralyzing moralism that sought justification by keeping the law. Later the Reformers found it necessary to protest the church's misplaced emphasis on the meritorious character of good works. More recently, modern liberalism, appealing to the "essential goodness" of human nature, preached the social gospel as the mark of true Christian living.

All these movements, and others, reflect a fundamental misunderstanding of the central message of the gospel. For this is the good news: In the death and resurrection of Christ, God justifies the ungodly by grace alone through faith, not of works, lest any man should boast. It is a gift of God. For while we were yet helplessly enslaved to sin, having forfeited every privilege, with nothing to commend us before God, under just condemnation, Christ took up our cause (Rom. 3:21-26; Eph. 2:4-9).

In view of man's built-in tendency to credit himself with some redeeming merit by which to lay claim upon God's favor, it is understandable that the Epistle to the Romans has played a vital role in almost every reformation in the history of the church.

1. What is there in human nature that accounts for this "do-it-yourself" religion cropping up again and again?

2. Explain the form in which this religious self-reliance appeared in Israel, in Pharisaism, in early Christian legalism, in Roman Catholicism, and in liberalism.

3. Why is the gospel of justification by grace alone a stumbling block to many of our contemporaries?

How to Get Right with God

All forms of self-justification are dead-end streets. Luther discovered this the hard way. Squarely he faced the basic question, How can a man get right with God? As a loyal son of the church he followed diligently the prescribed pattern of penance, pilgrimage, privation. But his afflicted conscience found no relief. Then one day, as he said, the windows of heaven (as it were) burst open and the light of the gospel broke through. He discovered anew that the righteousness of which the Bible speaks is not the righteousness that God *demands,* but the righteousness that He *gives.* Calvin was gripped by the same conviction, stating that justification by faith is "the main hinge on which religion turns." On this central point Calvin and Luther stand or fall together, and so the Calvinist has no trouble commemorating October 31 as ("Luther's") Reformation Day.

At stake was the believer's assurance of salvation. Roman Catholic tradition left men with a gnawing sense of insecurity. By encouraging men to attach some merit to their religious acts, the church wreaked havoc with faith and cast it into perpetual doubt. For who can ever be sure his penance is genuine enough and his good works meritorious enough? For Paul, indeed ("I know him whom I have believed, and I am persuaded . . ." II Tim. 1:12), and for the other apostles and a few saints, there is real assurance through special revelation. But the common Christian must spend his years in fear and trembling, hoping, praying, working for heaven's reward, but to his last breath caught in a ceaseless cycle of uncertainty.

Only by shunning every suggestion of self-justification, turning our eyes away from self and fixing them singly on Christ, only by affirming wholeheartedly that our justification depends wholly on God's unmerited favor can the Christian confess, "For I am persuaded, that . . . [nothing] shall be able to separate us from the love of God, which is in Christ Jesus our Lord" (Rom. 8:38, 39).

The Heidelberger puts it in these words: "God, without any merit of mine, of mere grace, grants and imputes to me the perfect satisfaction, righteousness, and holiness of Christ, as if I had never had nor committed any sin, and myself had accomplished all the obedience which Christ has rendered for me, if only I accept such benefit with a believing heart."

4. Should the work of Luther and Calvin be described as a reformation or as a revolution?
5. On what did Calvin and Luther agree and on what did they differ?
6. Why is the question of a right relationship to God of primary importance in our lives?
7. Should every Christian be able to make Paul's words of assurance his own?
8. How do you explain that "as if" in the answer of the Heidelberg Catechism?

Verdict: Not Guilty

Justification suggests a courtroom scene, where, in an almost incredible legal transaction, the Judge declares the guilty innocent. Not arbitrarily, capriciously, but justly and honestly. For this declaration of pardon is based on the most adequate and benevolent exchange in the world, that Christ became what He is not, a sinner, to make us what we are not, righteous. Therefore, reconciliation instead of recompense!

Undergirding the doctrine of justification are two other basic biblical doctrines. First, the doctrine of *substitution,* Christ's substitutionary atonement by which He took our place on Good Friday and Easter ("He was raised for our justification," Rom. 4:25). Secondly, the doctrine of *imputation,* by which the Father reckons to our account and the Holy Spirit brings home to us the full merits of Christ's finished work. This is the one and only sufficient, unending *justification* for our Christian faith and life.

The only worthiness demanded is a genuine sense of unworthiness, Calvin's humility, Luther's trust, every Christian's *faith.* Justified by faith alone! Faith is not intellectual assent to the doctrines of the church (Roman Catholicism), nor a leap in the dark (Barth), nor an emergency measure where reason fails (modernists), nor just a catechism answer (Reformed Christians all too often). Faith is self-denial, the rejection of all self-justification. It is a real, living, personal, unceasing confidence, not in my orthodoxy, nor in my personal piety, nor in my Christian witness, nor in my offerings, nor in my prayers, nor in my church-going, nor in my faith itself — but in Christ alone!

Scripture never denies that faith is a real act and a necessary response to God's grace. But it does strip faith of every modicum of merit. No one can boast of his "great faith," for boasting and believing are opposites. Faith is not a "work," slipping in at the last moment, adding a pinch of personal merit to the redemptive process. For then grace is no more grace.

Faith and justification: it is the correlation between these two that counts. Therefore, briefly stated: it is not merely faith *and* justification, but rather faith *in* God's justifying grace, and hence, justification *by* faith.

9. Is justification a single moment in our lives or a lifelong relation to God?

10. Is it right to speak of justification from eternity as well as justification by faith in history?

11. What is the function of faith in relationship to God's act of justification?

12. Is justification real and true to fact?

13. Are we in danger of trusting in our faith? What is wrong with this? Is faith a "work"?

Life of Sanctification — (19)

Romans 7:13-25; Philippians 3:7-15

The Christian Life

The sanctified life is, simply, yet profoundly stated, the whole range of the Christian life in all its everyday affairs. Living it faithfully is a job we work at full time. Putting it into words has been the concern of Christian thinkers in every age. Thomas a Kempis captured something of its mystic beauty in his book, *The Imitation of Christ*. Something of its trials and triumphs is picturesquely portrayed in the universal best seller, John Bunyan's *Pilgrim's Progress*. The deeply religious dimensions of it all find classic expression in John Calvin's *Golden Booklet of the True Christian Life* from the *Institutes*. Still, these all are but translations, for better or worse, of that call to sanctification which sounds from every page of Scripture.

A certain grocer had his finger on the pulsebeat of the Christian life when he placed this sign in his store window: "Live everyday as though Christ had died yesterday, arisen this morning, and were returning tomorrow." This is the atmosphere within which the Christian lives and moves and has his being. Life is religion, a faith-response to what God has done for us in Christ, and still does. Take "Christ" out of "Christian," and what is left isn't worth mentioning.

Sanctification is not a "new doctrine" which we take up after leaving justification behind. Neither in theory nor in practice, neither in our theological discussions nor in our life experience, may we break up the way of salvation into separate stages through which we pass one after another. The entire way of salvation is of one piece.

Yet sometimes we can get so entangled in questions about successive steps in the way of salvation — election, regeneration, calling (internal and external), justification, sanctification, glorification — that we lose sight of the biblical truth that our whole Christian life is really woven of a single redemptive fabric. Scripture teaches no fixed and rigid order of divine acts in our lives. Its consistent witness is this: that faith-fellowship with Christ brings us into faith-fellowship with all his benefits.

In Christ alone we are justified. And it is equally true that our sanctification is exclusively through him. We seek our whole salvation outside ourselves in Christ Jesus. The connecting link is always faith. By faith, in an irreversible moment, we are justified. By that same faith, moment by moment, we are sanctified. Hence justification is never a gateway through which we once pass, which then recedes steadily into the background. Just as the three parts of the Heidelberger — sin, salvation, and service — are not three successive stages through which we pass, first spending time with our sins, then dwelling on our salvation, and finally entering upon our service of sanctification. All three grow together into a deepening consciousness of our great salvation, full and free.

All along the line faith remains the abiding bond of fellowship. It is not one act among many in the way of salvation. It is rather the ever ongoing act of embracing the whole Christ with all his merits unto sanctification as well as justification. "The muscles of sanctity are attached to the tendons of faith" (Berkouwer).

1. In which ways do the three books mentioned above help us live the Christian life?

2. How do some people nowadays manage to deny Christ and still call themselves Christians?

3. In discussing the order of salvation, is it possible to so emphasize the **order** that the **salvation** escapes us?

4. Must we therefore conclude that all consideration of **order** in the way of salvation is immaterial?

5. What is the central function of faith all along the way in the Christian life?

The Art of Christian Living

Sanctification is life, and as all life, it grows. It throbs. It seeks to make progress. It fights the good fight in a life-and-death struggle, mortification and vivification, dying unto self and living anew unto Christ. Sanctification is for saints, those who have been set aside unto service to God. It makes for a basic difference among men. But it never allows for a sense of superiority. For who has attained? Learning the lessons of sanctification is an art for which even a lifetime is too short. It is only by devious twists and turns along the way that we make even the slightest progress. Growing in grace is never a kind of evolutionary process. Striving after holiness is never automatic. It is a tedious yet joyful progress, which always "keeps the windows of faith open to the grace of God" (Berkouwer).

A true sense of sanctification is the opponent of all hypocrisy. It cancels every feeling of having "arrived." For even the saintliest has still a long, long way to go. And he knows it better than anyone else. But he also knows that sin is no longer the master of his house. Sin is still a nasty backroom tenant, whose madness wreaks havoc. But his house is now under new management. Christ is the Landlord. Living in with him we discover new outlooks, new tastes, new habits moving us to at least a beginning of renewed obedience.

The tensions within us between sinfulness and sanctity can never be pressed into a mathematical formula, say 50/50 or 60/40 of virtue and vice. All the evil in me is of myself. All the good works in me are by faith in Christ. In myself I am wholly condemned: In Christ I am wholly sanctified. Yet the Spirit now works sanctification in me as my living response to God's wondrous grace. Not only in the upper room and inner closet. God's sanctifying grace touches life at every point, in courtship and marriage, in study and recreation, in buying and selling, and in all the rest. For sanctification is the lifelong re-creation of the whole creational life.

True sanctity shuns all pretense of piety, all parading of personal virtues, all theatrics, all playing to the galleries. It works in a secret, hidden way, as yeast in the lump of dough. Only God, who searches the heart, knows who is the saintliest among us all. After all, who manifested true sanctity, the rich with their handsome contributions, or the widow with her mite? Perhaps the saintliest among us lives somewhere on a rundown farm or lies on a forgotten sickbed — names that never appear in print.

6. How do you explain Paul's "pessimism" about the results of sanctification in his life (Rom. 7)?

7. Is it then consistent to hear notes of "optimism" coming from the same Paul in Philippians 3?

8. Are saintliness and sanctity reserved for a class of special Christians, such as monks, heroes of faith, missionaries?

9. Why is humility of the very essence of sanctification?

Winds of Doctrine

Heresy is often a distortion of some element of the truth. Throughout history there have been many distortions of the doctrine of sanctification.

Libertines argue that, if we are sanctified by faith in what Christ does for us, and not by our works, "So what?" if we live careless and reckless lives? Let us eat, drink, and be merry!

Passivists argue that, since our sanctification is taken up in our justification, and since both are accomplished outside of ourselves in Christ, then any further attempt at holiness on our part is bound to land us squarely in legalism and hypocrisy. Be that far from us! We will be content simply to receive what God has given us.

Moralism, mistaking the biblical call to "work out our own salvation," views good works as having an independent status, self-sponsored, cut loose from a wholehearted reliance on God's grace. We see it in the legalists of Paul's day, who sought a righteousness based on keeping the law. We see it in the mis-directed asceticism of medieval monks and saints. We see it in Christians who thought of the imitation of Christ in terms of duplicating the pattern of his holy life in theirs, regarding themselves as "little Christs." We see it in the empty platitudes of modernism, advocating a good life based on following the great Example.

Perhaps the boldest distortion of sanctification to appear in Christian circles is the "triumphant Christianity" of perfection-ism, with its strivings after a purist church, based on a "second blessing" granted to the spiritually elite. Since sanctification is a work of God, it must be perfect. Such perfection, though not actually attained by every Christian, remains a possibility and the ideal for all.

When all is said and done, it comes down to this: Scripture never discredits earnest activity. Strive to enter in! But it does cancel every notion of personal merit attached to programs of self-improvement.

We must increasingly *become* what we *are*. We are Christians, aren't we? Then we must more steadfastly and consistently become Christian in our total way of life.

10. What biblical answer can you offer to each distortion of the truth sketched above?

11. Why are a true sense of sanctification and the pretense of personal merit opposed to each other?

12. What are the implications of the biblical call to **become** what we **are?**

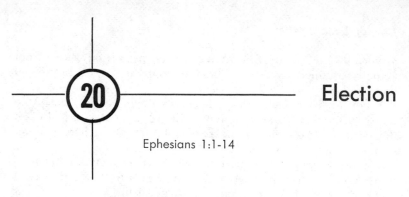

Election

Ephesians 1:1-14

Caricature

The man on the street seems always to equate Calvinism with predestination. And for him this is reason enough to reject it. For who wants to serve a divine Despot, who, without batting an eyelash, carries out this "horrible decree" (Calvin!) by capriciously dividing all mankind into sheep and goats? And all this before any man ever saw the light of day! With disdain or indignation he will declare that he has no room for a doctrine which teaches "that God, by a mere arbitrary act of his will, without the least respect or view to any sin, has predestined the greater part of the world to eternal damnation, and has created them for this very purpose" (rejected in the Canons of Dort). Be done with such a religion of tyranny and fatalistic submission to a harsh and inexorable Will!

In this emotional outburst we face a popular, yet real, caricature of this article of faith. What a ganglion of prejudices! A rock of offense, a stone of stumbling! Deliberate distortion, too! But how often haven't we by our thoughtless "preaching" or inconsistent "practice" lent support to these false notions? The conviction of divine election often adorns our lives quite ungraciously, and we live with it uncomfortably, instead of drawing from it and conveying by it the comfort and joy which accompanies the biblical witness to this assurance of our salvation. Too often we treat it as a "problem." We view it as a dark cloud which hangs menacingly over our heads, eclipsing the full sunshine of God's grace and love.

Calvin faced these very difficulties in his day. There were the overly cautious, who, baffled by the mystery of it all, said it was best "to avoid any question of it, as we would a reef." There were also the overly curious, who, by their unrestrained speculations, rashly penetrated "the sacred precincts of divine wisdom," thus entering "a labyrinth from which they can find no exit." Now as then, Calvin's advice is sound: hold to the Word of God, no more, no less. "I desire only to have them admit that we should not investigate what the Lord has left hidden in secret, that we should not neglect what He has brought into the open, so that we may not be convicted of excessive curiosity on the one hand, or of excessive ingratitude on the other."

1. Why do hosts of people resent so deeply and react so violently to the doctrine of election?

2. What do you think Calvin meant in calling election a "horrible decree"? What meaning did the word "horrible" have at that time?

3. Are we guilty of misleading people by our confession and conduct with respect to this Biblical teaching?

4. Are there the overly cautious and overly curious among us too?

5. Is obsessive and fearful concern with the decree of election a source of psychiatric problems?

Eternity

Children often use a playful formula for eliminating partners from a game: "Eeny, meeny, miny, mo . . . and out you go!" Adults sometimes take a similar attitude toward God's eternal decrees, as though everything were "settled" in advance. But the Bible never presents God's act of election as a cold and dispassionate decision, which demands of us that we somehow enter into the eternal mind of God to determine where we stand with him.

Scripture never invites us to a theological bull session, where we speculate wildly about the relation of time and eternity in order to unveil some secret ground for our Christian faith. The Bible sees no conflict between election from eternity ("before the foundation of the world") and election here and now ("in Christ"). For God is ever the same, yesterday, today, and tomorrow. He is true to himself and faithful to us. He does not lead us to faith, only to shake that faith by giving us a glimpse into the wellspring of his mercy from which his electing love flows to us. By turning our eyes to his everlasting love He intends to steady our trust by pointing to the source of our salvation.

The secret things belong to God, whereas the revealed things are for us and our children (Deut. 29:29). Often we give the impression that our election belongs to the secret things. But even this act of God's inscrutable wisdom is ours. By faith we embrace Christ and *all* his benefits. Therefore, after settling the question of faith-hope-love, we may not turn to election as a "new question" yet to be settled. For Christ is the final and ultimate answer to every last question in life, for time and eternity. Belief in God's electing love must drive away all our lingering doubts about our call to Christian service.

6. Does God's self-revelation in Scripture allow for a view of election as an arbitrary and capricious act?

7. For what reason does the Bible reveal to us something of the eternal depths of our salvation in the decree of election?

8. Should a confession of our election lead us to complacency? carelessness? confidence?

Christ

Sometimes it is said that *first* the Father chose to elect some from the fallen human race, and *then* Christ was commissioned to carry out this decision — as though our election was only *through* Christ, but not *in* Christ. Or again it has been said that the Father was moved by his righteous judgment to view us with disfavor; but that the Son, moved by compassion for us, changed the Father's vengeful mood to a friendly disposition — as though there was disharmony within the Trinity. Both of these notions are in sharp conflict with Paul's word, "God was in Christ reconciling the world unto himself" (II Cor. 5:19). If Christ be *for* us, how could the Father in any sense be *against* us?

Indeed, there is no higher being or higher law to which God is subject or to which God must give account. His election rests in his good pleasure. But his good pleasure is not a willy-nilly affair, but an expression of his trustworthiness and faithfulness. Despairing of any grounds for benevolence in ourselves, all our considerations of election must begin and end in the Father's love and in the grace of our Lord Jesus Christ.

Christ is the manifestation of God's mercy. He is the "mirror· of our election" (Calvin). Do you want surety concerning God's electing love for you? Then look in the Mirror! What more can God say than He has said in his Son! If we have seen Christ, then we have seen the Father (John 14:7). The God of election is the same God who comes to us in Christ.

It is therefore futile to seek assurance by taking some mystical detour, bypassing the appointed Way, presuming thus to establish a more direct contact with the Father. For there is one Mediator of election, Christ Jesus. And no one comes to the Father except through him (John 14:6). Belief in election is not something in addition to faith in Christ. Nor is the Christ-revelation a compensation for the concealment which enshrouds the mystery of election; for this mystery is fully revealed in Christ. Nor is faith in Christ provisional, awaiting and dependent upon a further revelation, namely a voice from heaven or a voice at the end of the road. For in Christ God has proclaimed his decisive "yes" (II Cor. 1:20).

9. Why is it wrong to suggest any disharmony within the Trinity in the work of redemption?

10. Can we do justice to the doctrine of election if we discuss it under the doctrine of God prior to a study of the person and work of Christ?

11. According to the Bible, what does it mean to be "in Christ"?

12. Does the Bible offer any grounds for thinking that divine election is based on foreknowledge?

Others

Standing in the grace of God's electing love, what shall we say about the others, the non-elect, the reprobates? As the church preaches the gospel of God's gracious election unto assurance and joy, so, in unfolding the full counsel of God's Word, it must with heaviness of heart also proclaim God's rejection of those who reject him unto urgent warning and appeal. Kiss the Son ("in Christ") lest you perish in the way!

The responsibility for a reprobate heart lies with man. God is in no sense the author of evil. Moreover, He is not the cause and fountain of unbelief "in the same manner" (Canons of Dort) that He is the cause and fountain of faith. Reprobation is neither a wholly autonomous act of man (for it too finds a place in the eternal decree of God) nor is it causally traceable back to God's will. It is somehow *within* the will of God, and *contrary* to it, but not *according* to it. Behold the mystery of iniquity! Every attempt to trace the cause of one's sin back beyond oneself to an eternal divine decision is an attempt to shift the burden of one's guilt upon God. Election is undeserved favor. Reprobation is well-deserved judgment. The only way of escape in this labyrinthian way is to seek refuge in the freely offered electing love of that God who in Christ has given his standing promise:

"Seek ye the Lord while he may be found;
   call ye upon him while he is near;
   let the wicked forsake his way,
   and the unrighteous man his thoughts;
   and let him return unto Jehovah,
   and he will have mercy upon him;
   and to our God,
   for he will abundantly pardon" — *Isa. 55:6, 7*

13. What does it mean that God is not the cause and fountain of reprobation "in the same manner" as He is of election?

14. Why is it wrong to pin the responsibility for sin on anyone but ourselves?

15. What can we learn from David's prayer, "Cast me not away" (Ps. 51:11)?

16. What value should we place on "the evidences of election" (Calvin) in our lives?

17. What can we learn about the relation of election and missions from Acts 13:48?

18. How can we "strive to make our calling and election sure" (II Peter 1:10)?

Christian Freedom ⎯⎯⎯⎯ (21)

I Corinthians 8, 9

Liberty, Law, and Tyranny

"Freedom" is everybody's creed these days. In recent history we have experienced the quest for freedom on every hand: the "Freedom Fighters" of Hungary, "Freedom Riders" in the southern United States, "religious liberty" discussed at the Second Vatican Council, debates on the "right-to-work laws" in the U.S. Congress, and Cubans pouring into Florida in search of freedom.

Freedom is also a central theme in the Christian gospel. "Where the Spirit of the Lord is, there is liberty" (II Cor. 3:17). For "if the Son shall make you free, ye shall be free indeed" (John 8:36). "Stand fast therefore in the liberty wherewith Christ hath made us free" (Gal. 5:1, A.V.). These are New Testament translations of the Old Testament message of liberation, "I am Jehovah thy God, who brought thee out of the land of Egypt" (Exod. 20:1).

In a deeply religious sense Patrick Henry's cry, "Give me liberty, or give me death," is everybody's business. Bondage or freedom: this is the only choice we have. It is a question of being under the awful indictment of God's law, or under the liberating rule of his grace. To know the exhilarating power of the canceled debt of sin is freedom in the deepest sense of the word.

Through the first Adam we all became enslaved to Satan and sin and self. Satan is a terrible taskmaster. Sin is slavery. Self-will is tyranny. In the last Adam, however, the shackles have been broken. Christ is our Liberator. Yes, He is also our Lord, for we are not our own, but belong to him (Heidelberg Catechism, I). But this Master reassures us, "My yoke is easy, and my burden is light" (Matt. 11:30).

For every man there comes the moment of decision: choose you this day whom you will serve! For every man needs a master. And no man can really serve *two* masters. Serving some creature is bondage. Serving the Creator is freedom. Note well the paradox: the servant is the freeman. Freedom and service go hand in hand.

The medieval church subjected the layman to the hierarchy, robbing him of his Christian liberty by enslaving him to human traditions. Only by a soul-stirring struggle did the Reformers rediscover the word of Christ: "Ye shall know the truth, and the truth shall make you *free*" (John 8:32). That was the moment of release: freedom from works-righteousness, freedom from the ensnaring tentacles of an octopus-like church, freedom to serve God in all the callings of life without a guilty conscience for by-passing the monastery or the nunnery.

Justification by faith, says Calvin, "is the main hinge on which religion turns," and Christian freedom is "a special appendage to justification." Standing on the righteousness of Christ, not on our attempts to keep the law, we enjoy a free conscience before God, and also before our fellowmen, even though our lives fall far short of the mark.

1. How can we explain the fact that all men have an inner urge to be free?

2. In what sense is a self-seeking person a slave?

3. How can we reconcile liberty and law? freedom and service?

4. Can you describe historically how the Reformers rediscovered the biblical call to freedom?

5. How are justification by faith and Christian freedom related?

6. Can you explain how Luther could possibly say, "Sin bravely"?

Liberty, License, and Service

But aren't we playing here with dynamite? Yes, freedom can easily be lost. But freedom can just as easily be turned into license. We must, of course, face up to the fact that the truth is always dangerous. Some have charged that this freedom makes men "careless and profane" (Heidelberg Catechism, XXIV), that it destroys all moderation, turns some men into Libertines and others into Pharisees. Shall we then drop the whole matter from our Christian vocabulary and life to avoid trouble? This would be a blow at the very heart of the gospel.

For justification by faith and Christian freedom stand and fall together. Christian freedom is our moral response to the reality of our justification by faith. Religion and morals, faith and life are inseparable.

The so-called "new morality" has forced upon our generation a renewed consideration of this whole question. The byword of this current movement is *freedom*. Its appeal is to *love*. But it is love without *law*. Love must be free, it is argued, or else it is not love. The only law is love itself. This modern libertinism has generated a wave of "new morality" (or "not-so-new immorality") which is now sweeping through our university campuses.

Defining Christian freedom more carefully, it is, first of all, freedom *from* the law as a demanding taskmaster requiring us to keep the law in order to earn salvation. This was the big issue in Christ's running encounter with the Pharisees. But it is also freedom *unto* the law as a rule of gratitude to be willingly obeyed and spontaneously lived as the law of love to God and fellowmen. Freedom *from* and freedom *unto*: such freedom spells the difference between slavery and sonship. Slaves cower before their masters. Sons, on the other hand, "do not hesitate to offer to their fathers incomplete and half-done and even defective works, trusting that their obedience and readiness of mind will be accepted by their fathers, even though they have not quite achieved what their fathers intended" (Calvin). What counts ultimately is this: whether one's *heart* is in the right place.

Making choices in life between things clearly good-and-right and things clearly bad-and-wrong is quite easy. But in between is a whole area of difficult decisions on things neither good nor bad, neither right nor wrong in themselves (Calvin's *adiaphora*). Such things are good or bad, right or wrong, depending on how we use them. For example, the clothes we wear, the food we eat, the hours we keep, watching TV, using cosmetics. What we do with these things does not decide our relation to God. Our proper use of them is not a question of *faith* toward God, but of *love* toward our fellowmen. It is the motivation and application that counts.

7. How can we misuse our freedom?
8. How do you react to the so-called "new morality"?

9. What is the thrust of I Peter 2:16?

10. How do you explain David's doxology, "O how love I thy law"?

11. Explain in which ways we are free in the use of "indifferent" things.

Liberty, Love, and Wisdom

We must use Christian wisdom in exercising our Christian freedom, for we face two great dangers. First, many turn liberty into licentious living by unprincipled and undisciplined indulgence in secular pleasures. Calvin, a very practical theologian, observed that "there is almost no one whose resources permit him to be extravagant who does not delight in lavish and ostentatious banquets, bodily apparel, and domestic architecture; who does not wish to outstrip his neighbors in all sorts of elegance; who does not wondrously flatter himself in his opulence." How up to date! Keeping up with the Joneses, status seeking, the spirit of suburbia — these are signs of our times. All this in the name of Christian freedom. But it was Paul who said: learn contentment, live in moderation. All things are lawful for me, but not all things are helpful.

A second danger is offending others by our exercise of Christian freedom. Our liberty before God does not allow us to be unconcerned about the feelings of other Christians, especially the "weaker brethren." No one may flaunt his fellows by boldly parading or arrogantly displaying his free spirit. Christian liberty makes us as free to abstain as to indulge. The law of love must dictate our use of the rule of liberty.

The "weaker brother" must, however, be distinguished from the fault-finding hypocrite. Christ himself, setting us an example, was all compassion toward the common people. But He seems to go out of his way to step on the long toes of the Pharisees. There is a difference between *giving* offense and *taking* offense. We must curtail our freedom rather than give offense to sensitive Christians. But, on the other hand, we may not allow carping critics who seek occasion for taking offense to rob us of our freedom. Yet in it all, neither the "weaker brother" nor the hypocrite, but rather God's free grace remains the standard for the exercise of our liberty.

This points to the context for our liberty: *freedom* within the law of *love,* and all within the framework of *faith.* Never do anything in the name of freedom that violates our obligation to "owe no man anything, but to love one another" (Rom. 13:8). Never in turn do anything in the name of the law of love that violates the faith we owe to God. Freedom is the servant of love to our neighbor and faith to God.

12. Do you think Christians are guilty of violating Christian freedom by over-indulging in things which are good in themselves?

13. Can you think of cases in which we offend "weaker brethren"?

14. Why should we treat self-righteous hypocrites differently from weaker brethren?

15. What lesson does Paul leave us in I Corinthians 8:13?

16. How are freedom and love and faith interrelated?

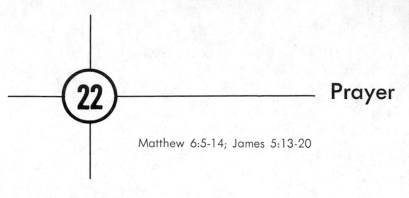

22 — Prayer

Matthew 6:5-14; James 5:13-20

Communion and Communication

During the interview following his historic flight into space, John Glenn was asked whether he prayed much during those perilous moments in orbit. "No," he replied, "I don't believe in 'fire-truck religion'; I did my praying beforehand!"

Prayer is not an emergency measure. It is the Christian's "vital breath," his "native air." It is a running conversation, with crescendos and pauses, between Christian children and their heavenly Father. It is both communion and communication.

Too often, however, we think of prayer merely as religious *devotion,* not as a biblical *doctrine,* not as a subject for serious theological discussion, but as a lighter topic for an after-recess program. Perhaps our theologians have misled us on this point. In modern times most books on systematic theology have not included a treatment of the doctrine of prayer. Not so with John Calvin, who left us a beautiful chapter on prayer in his *Institutes.* Here are a few excerpts: "Just as faith is born from the gospel, so through faith our hearts are trained to call upon God's name. . . . For by prayer we dig up the treasures that are pointed out by the Lord's gospel, and which our faith has gazed upon. . . . So it remains for us to seek in God, and in prayer to ask of Him, what we have learned to be in Him. . . . Let us then remember that this is the message of Divine Wisdom [on prayer], teaching what it wills and willing what is needful" (*Institutes,* III, 20).

Martin Luther literally wore out his rug kneeling in prayer. Without four hours of prayer daily, he felt the Reformation would be a lost cause. David Livingstone said, "In missions we make our greatest advances upon our knees."

It is no wonder, then, that demonic forces try to close the

windows of prayer. For, outlaw prayer, and the lifeline is broken. Therefore Daniel had no choice but to defy the king's order in keeping the two-way traffic with God flowing freely (Dan. 6:6-10).

No one needed prayer so little, yet so much, as Christ. So little, being himself the Answer to prayer. So much, being elected for us to make the impossible possible. His example puts us to shame: a whole night in prayer (Luke 6:12), sweating it out in agonizing prayer in the garden (Luke 22:44), and at Golgotha crucifying himself to his Father's will in a final prayer of perfect self-surrender (Luke 23:46).

Prayer is not light exercise. It is hard work. Indeed, it is a great privilege and a gratifying experience. But it is also a serious responsibility and a demanding challenge. We sense this in the disciples' request, "Lord, teach us to pray" (Luke 11:1). Replying, Christ does not say: "Any old way will do." Prayer is not a hit-and-miss affair. It demands discipline. Therefore Christ leaves his disciples, then and now, the perfect prayer as a pattern to follow. The purpose of the Lord's Prayer is to teach "that no man should ask for, expect, or demand anything at all except what is included, by way of summary, in this prayer; and though the words may be completely different, yet the meaning ought not to vary" (Calvin).

1. Was Mr. Glenn's answer right? Why?
2. Do you think we have lost something since Calvin in omitting prayer from our books on Christian doctrine?
3. What does Hebrews 11:6 teach about faith as the foundation of prayer?
4. Do you think that Luther and Livingstone were overdoing a good thing?
5. How can we as Christians serve as the intercessors for our society (as Abraham for Sodom and Stephen for Jerusalem)?
6. Can you explain what prayer must have meant for Christ?
7. In which ways must our prayer life be disciplined?

Three Trouble Spots

In reflecting on our prayers we face three knotty problems. First, if God is *omniscient*, and therefore knows our needs before we even express them, and knows them better than we can present them, isn't it really unnecessary to pray? Why tell God what He already knows! But, as Calvin says, "the Lord ordained prayer not so much for his sake as for ours." Not that prayer is simply a religious therapeutic exercise. It is fellowship with God, and as in any fellowship, the conversation drifts to familiar things. We talk with God as a child with his father: though the father knows very well what the child wants, yet the child just can't help talking to his father about it.

Second, if God is *immutable*, why pray? We can't change God's unchangeable plan, can we? This objection forces us to face the basic question: by what standard are we to live? By God's secret will or by his revealed will? God's revelation is clear: "Pray without ceasing" (I Tim. 5:17). Our prayers themselves are part of God's unchanging plan. Moreover, prayer *does* change things. Elijah prayed first for drought, then for rain, and his prayers were answered.

Third, since Christ said, "Seek, and ye shall find" (Matt. 7:7), what shall we say about those *unanswered prayers?* Paul prayed thrice to be relieved of the thorn in his flesh, but to no avail. To no avail? "My grace is sufficient for you, for my strength is made perfect in weakness" (II Cor. 12:9). God never turns a deaf ear to earnest prayer. For "my prayer is more certainly heard of God than I feel in my heart that I desire these things of Him" (Heidelberg Catechism, No. 129).

8. Study carefully these three objections and explore more fully what light Scripture casts upon these questions.

9. Do you think faith healing is possible through prayer?

Ora et Labora

Prayer, standing alone, is the empty echo of a hollow heart. True prayer is our answer to God's Word. Therefore Bible reading and prayerful response go hand in hand. We come to God in prayer because He has first come to us in his revelation. Scripture readings themselves are often the very best prayers.

In sketching the life of Christian gratitude, the Heidelberg Catechism begins with the law as the rule of thanks-living and ends with prayer as "the chief part of the thankfulness which God requires of us." Prayer is not an option, but a question of obedience; not a matter of convenience, but a command. Precept and prayer go hand in hand, prayer being, as it were, the soul, and keeping God's commands the body. Therefore, prayer without keeping God's commands is a ghost. And keeping God's commands without the spirit of prayer is a corpse. Prayer is both spontaneous *obedience* and obedient *spontaneity.*

Furthermore, faith and prayer, without works, are dead. Prayer can never serve as a substitute for Christian work. It is the atmosphere in which we work. Rising from our knees we put our shoulders to the wheel. The spirit of our prayers takes on flesh and blood and bones in the way we live. *Ora* leads to *labora,* and *labora* must be consistent with *ora,* "so that," as a classic marriage form says, "your prayers may not be hindered" (cf. Isa. 1:15). It may be downright wrong to fold our hands and close our eyes when somewhere in the Christian community the call to action is sounded. For we insult God when we pray, "Thy kingdom come," unless we at the same time make ourselves available as willing instruments in God's hand.

We often say our prayers, but do we really pray? Imperfect prayers! Even our prayers for forgiveness need God's forgiving grace. But you say, "I can't pray nice"? Remember, it is really not the nicety of the words that counts. God listens for the heart behind the words, just as an understanding mother reads the mind of her lisping, stammering child.

Sometimes, groping in darkness, prayer becomes the path by which we find our way back to the God whom we thought we had lost. Sometimes our prayers run dry. Sometimes desire fails. Then Satan's temptation is fiercest, when he says, "Don't pray unless you feel like it, for otherwise you're a hypocrite." This is the death of prayer. Scripture replies, Don't stop! For our prayer appetite grows in the way of obedience. Sometimes words fail us; we don't know what to pray for. Then we must still pray until we rediscover our real needs and God's will for our lives. At such moments it is reassuring to know that Christ prays for us, and the Holy Spirit, too, intercedes for us with groanings that cannot be uttered.

The only limits are these: pray according to God's revealed will. Just as a child refrains from asking certain things of his parents, because he senses that these things would be contrary to their whole way of life, so some things should never find their way into our prayers, inasmuch as we sense that to request these gifts would be to flout the Giver.

10. How is prayer related to the Word? to God's commands? to our daily good works?

11. Do you agree with Calvin that the church should be "repeatedly stirred up to more frequent use of prayer and fired by a sharper zeal if it is alerted to some major need"?

12. Do you ever think of congregational singing as a kind of musical praying?

13. Do you feel, as Calvin does, that our public prayers are often too long and our private prayers often too short?

14. What lesson in prayer can we learn from the parable of the widow and the judge (Luke 18:1-8)?

15. From the parable of the publican and the Pharisee (Luke 18:9-14)?

16. Should prayers be at stated times, or spontaneous?

17. How important is it, for the sake of our children, that we pray aloud at the table?

The Marks of the Church

Matthew 18:15-20; II Timothy 4:1-8

Schism or Reform

The Protestantism of the sixteenth century: was it *revolution* or *reformation?* There is, after all, a world of difference between the two. Take Luther and Calvin: were they reformers or rebels? It has been common practice during past centuries for Roman Catholic writers to decry the warped personalities and the malicious intents of the reformers. They were schismatics and heretics. Nowadays, however, these highly prejudiced pictures are being reviewed and revised in favor of a more charitable judgment, "Separated brethren!"

Luther, pioneer of the Reformation, and Calvin, second generation mastermind of the Reformation, both launched their careers as loyal sons of the church. Only after discovering by long and hard and bitter experience that Rome had closed its mind to serious change, only then did these reformers enter upon the open road of Reformation by separation and exclusion.

To sever relations with his spiritual mother was for Calvin a painful experience. This is his testimony: "I was not easily extricated from that miry pit," but "God laid his heavy hand on me". . . ."the Almighty reduced my heart to teachableness." Not until he was convinced that taking this step was reform, not schism, was he ready to make his move. Two factors made it especially difficult for him. First, in all his thinking and living Calvin was an orderly man, opposed to anarchy and chaos. Hence church reforms too must be undertaken "decently and in good order." Second, Calvin's high view of the church compelled him to consider his ways carefully before reconstituting it. After all, the church is the body of Christ. Woe to him who lightly dismembers that body!

By what standard then shall we distinguish between the true church and the false church? Between true churches and false churches? Between reformers and schismatics? The Belgic Confession in Article 28 offers us these guidelines: "The true Church must be distinguished from all sects that call themselves the Church by these three marks: if the pure doctrine of the gospel is preached therein; if it maintains the pure administration of the sacraments as instituted by Christ; if church discipline is exercised in punishing sin; in short, if all things are managed according to the pure Word of God, all things contrary thereto are rejected, and Jesus Christ acknowledged as the only Head of the Church. Hereby the true Church may certainly be known, from which no man has a right to separate himself."

This was the standard of judgment in the sixteenth-century Reformation, and in other Protestant reformations since then. But it works both ways. Taking seriously the sin of schism, some Christians have felt obliged to remain members of degenerate churches, living there in vocal or silent protest against ongoing processes of deformation (Arminianism, Liberalism, Barthianism). Others, seriously applying the marks of the church, have repeatedly sounded the call to reformation, declaring that they had to leave the existing church in order to return to the true church.

The three marks do not provide us with an easy formula for separating the sheep from the goats, but a dynamic, scripturally embedded touchstone by which to test the spirits whether they be of God or not. It is not always easy to determine in what sense and measure a given denomination represents the true church. Every church falls short of the high calling of God in Christ.

Recognizing this, the Reformed churches have repeatedly resisted the perfectionistic tendencies of Spiritualists who enforced a purist church ideal, a communion composed solely of elite believers. For the purity of the church is not to be judged by the holiness of its members, but by the presence in principle and practice of the three marks. Hence Calvin's position, that though the lives of the people of a given church swarm with evils, this does not in itself warrant separation. On this point he practiced what he preached, advising the Christians

of Geneva to remain loyal to their church, even though it had
banished Calvin himself and tolerated questionable conduct,
for the marks of the church were not absent.

1. What is the difference between schism and reform? Give an
   example of each.
2. How do you account for the fact that Roman Catholicism is
   changing its judgment upon Protestants from "heretics and
   schismatics" to "separated brethren"?
3. Do you think we take the high biblical view of the church as
   seriously as the Reformers did?
4. If church membership is a "marriage contract," as Calvin says,
   may we ever file for a "divorce" from the church?
5. How must we conceive of the relationship between God's **one**
   church and our **many** churches?
6. What is wrong with insisting on a "perfect church"?
7. Can you think of a situation where it would be justifiable
   to stick with a degenerate church?

Test of Truth

The three marks are not a rigid rule of thumb by which to
classify all churches once and for all as true or false, more
or less. Rather, they provide a living, dynamic standard of
judgment, applicable to changing circumstances. We cannot,
for example, conduct a survey and grade one church as 75
percent true and another 50 percent true, for good. Instead,
on a given Sunday, in a given church (even a reputedly "lax
church"), if the Word is clearly and convincingly preached,
then at that time and place the church came to real and true
manifestation. The next Sunday, if the pulpit offers stones for
bread, it may then be next to impossible to sense the presence
of the true church.

We are surrounded these days by many churches that
have long ago removed the hallmarks of the Christian faith.
Still, well-meaning Christians stick with such churches for historical or sentimental reasons. Our hearts are deceitful. We are
all given to rationalizations. Nor is sincerity an adequate test
of rightness, for men can be sincerely wrong. Therefore the
Reformed Confession prescribes three biblical marks as norms

for evaluating the rightness or wrongness, truth or falsity, purity or impurity of the church's faith and life.

Not every religious organization is a church. In Canada and the United States there are more than four hundred recognizable denominations, plus countless religious rackets and fly-by-night affairs. Besides degenerate and false churches, there are "peoples' churches" which throw the doors wide open to every wind of doctrine, and sects which make a career out of religious fantasies. In this ecclesiastical madhouse a Christian who takes the church seriously needs a reliable standard for making sound judgments if he is to retain his sanity.

8. How would you apply the marks of the church to your local congregation?

9. What is the difference between a church and a sect?

10. Does a Christian bear corporate responsibility for the principles and practices of his church, whether good or bad?

11. How do you account for the proliferation of religious bodies in America?

Discipline

The Bible does not give us a ready-made *doctrine* of the three marks of the church. But it does give us the *revealed truths* that we then assemble into a doctrine. The writings of the New Testament call the church purely to preach the gospel (I John 1:1-4), rightly to administer the sacraments (I Cor. 11:17-34), and faithfully to conduct Christian discipline (I Cor. 5:1-5).

The Belgic Confession, drawing heavily on Calvin's thinking, witnesses clearly to the threefold mark of the church. Yet Calvin himself usually speaks of only two marks, the Word and the sacraments. Not that Calvin overlooked discipline. He, in fact, insists upon it emphatically as the instrument for keeping the Word and the sacraments alive and effective in the church.

The history of Protestantism is a pointed confirmation of the rightness of Calvin's emphasis. Many churches have discarded discipline, only to discover that then the Word soon loses its power and the sacraments their meaningfulness. Church discipline — admonition and exhortation, encouragement and con-solation — is the effective means for maintaining the character of the church's calling and for individualizing the message of the Word and the sacraments (more on this in the following chapter) as means of grace.

It is clear from Scripture that the church must exercise its discipline not by might nor by power, but by the persuasive force of the Word and sacraments. This is the only sword it wields. That sword must be used in the name of Christ, in submission to the Spirit, with loving and patient concern, combining firmness with tenderheartedness. What goals must we keep in mind? Two: first, by mutual admonition and the pastoral work of the elders, the Christian community seeks to win back its wayward and rebellious children and to build each other up in the Christian faith. Second, by its discipline the church must demonstrate its loyalty to its Lord and its faithfulness to its calling, both in its preaching and in its practice. The church exists ultimately for God's sake, not for ours; for his honor, and for our salvation.

12. Is missions a separate mark of the church?

13. How are the three marks related to each other?

14. How would you explain the decline of church discipline among Protestant churches?

15. Try to present a sample case to illustrate how the church should exercise discipline aright.

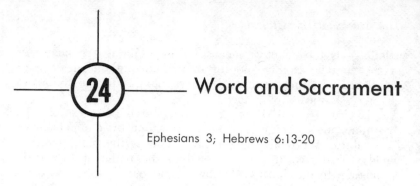

Word and Sacrament

Our Spiritual Mother

The church is the mother of believers (Gal. 4:26). Accordingly, Christians in every age have appealed to the words of Augustine, "I would not have God as my Father, unless I had the Church as my mother." Calvin puts it this way: "For there is no other way to enter into life unless this mother conceive us in her womb, give us birth, nourish us at her breast, and keep us under her care and guidance. . . . Our weakness does not allow us to be dismissed from her school until we have been pupils all our lives" (*Institutes*, IV, 1, 4).

The church has been entrusted with two tools or aids, the two means of grace, namely, the Word and the sacraments. In proclaiming the Word and administering the sacraments, the church fulfills its role as the servant of all God's servants. Through this double means of grace, the Holy Spirit — who indwells the church — exercises his sovereign power in the world. The Word and sacraments are his chief instruments unto conversion and sanctification.

Through the church we receive a triple blessing. "For first, the Lord teaches and instructs us by his Word. Secondly, he confirms the Word by the sacraments. Finally, he illumines our minds by his Holy Spirit and opens our hearts for the Word and sacraments to enter in, which would otherwise only strike our ears and appear before our eyes, but not at all affect us within" (Calvin, *Institutes*, IV, 14, 8).

Shut down the church, and the Word will be silenced, and faith will die. For faith cometh by hearing, and hearing by the Word of God, and the Word by preaching, and preaching by the church that sends out its heralds (Rom. 10:14-17).

The Word of Scripture arose out of the life of the church.

But, more deeply, the life of the church springs from the regenerating and reforming power of the Word. The church must therefore submit itself to the Word, to which it owes its existence, and thus pursue its calling to handle aright the Word of truth (II Tim. 2:15).

The Word is self-authenticating. Its authority does not depend on the endorsement of the church, as Roman Catholicism teaches. Yet, in its preaching and teaching, the church does exercise a pedagogical authority. As a mother she introduces us to the message of the Bible.

The Word of God has four dimensions to it. There is, first, the Word originally revealed to the prophets and apostles with an authoritative ring, "Thus saith the Lord!" These redemptive messages were then committed to writing in the Holy Scriptures under the guidance of the Holy Spirit. In the fullness of time this Word of God became flesh and dwelt among us in Christ Jesus. Now it remains the ongoing task of the church to translate this Word into the language of all men everywhere. Thus we now have the revealed Word, the written Word, the incarnate Word, the preached Word — but in all its manifestations, the Word of God!

1. Develop as fully as you can the biblical idea of the church as the "mother of believers."

2. Show how this biblical idea expresses itself differently in the Roman Catholic Church than in the churches of the Reformation.

3. How do you explain the constant temptation on the part of the church to "lord it over the flock"?

4. What is the difference between the work of the Holy Spirit in **inspiring** the writing of Scripture and **illuminating** our minds to receive it?

5. How does the church as our spiritual mother exercise her pedagogical authority?

6. Should sermons be for children too?

Signed and Sealed

The church must sow the seed of God's Word in every soil; to every nation, tongue, and race; to "insiders" and "outsiders," to believers and unbelievers alike. But the sacraments are for Christians only. We may erect our pulpits anywhere, on street corners, in TV stations, all over creation. But the sacraments belong up front in church, in the circle of believers, whether in a cathedral or along the hedgerows, whether in a chapel or at the water's edge.

Sacraments are redemptive symbols, signs and seals of God's grace in Christ Jesus. Israel's religion was enriched by two sacraments: circumcision and passover. In both there was blood-letting, foreshadowing the crimson tide of Calvary. Both stood in the shadows of the great "not yet." In Christ at last the old became new, not by discarding the old, but by absorbing it forever into the new. The upper room marked the transition from the passover to the Lord's Supper. In the Great Commission circumcision makes way for baptism.

Between the old and the new there is a strong sacramental *continuity*: both circumcision and baptism represent initiation into the community of believers, and both passover and communion represent full fellowship within that community. But there is also *discontinuity*: the transforming power of the cross is the bridge spanning the gulf between Judaism and Christianity. Yet, in the old by way of expectation, and in the new by way of fulfillment, the focal point of the sacraments is Christ Jesus, the one Mediator between God and man.

7. How do you explain the fact that sacraments are for Christians only, whereas the Word reaches out to all men?

8. What are the similarities and differences between Old Testament sacraments and New Testament sacraments?

9. On what basis do Roman Catholics argue for seven New Testament sacraments instead of two?

Primary and Secondary

Having these *two* means of grace does not mean that we have *two* ways of salvation. For they are but *two* instruments in the hand of the *one* Spirit, "the inward Teacher," who uses a *duality* of means to bring us unto the *unity* of faith. "If the Spirit be lacking, the sacraments can accomplish nothing more in our minds than the splendor of the sun shining upon blind eyes, or a voice sounding in deaf ears. Therefore I make such a distinction between Spirit and sacraments that the power to act rests with the former, and the ministry alone is left to the latter — a ministry empty and trifling apart from the action of the Spirit, but charged with great effect when the Spirit works within and manifests his power" (*Institutes,* IV, 14, 9). The church of the Middle Ages and modern Roman Catholicism accentuated the sacraments at the expense of the Word. Preaching was at best a preparation for sacramental grace. Recently, however, the Church of Rome has begun to recover something of the central significance of the Word in the life of the church. Meanwhile many Protestant churches have gradually drifted away from the centrality of the Word in favor of a greater sacramental and liturgical emphasis.

The Reformers believed the Word was *primary,* the sacraments *secondary.* The Word can stand alone, but not the sacraments. For the sacraments depend upon the Word for their meaning. The elements without the Word of interpretation are mere "magic." Both are *equally* dependent on the sovereign power of the Spirit. And both *alike* become ours only by faith. But, by scriptural definition, they are not of equal value.

Preaching is God's *audible* Word, the sacraments his *visible* and *tangible* Word. The one is not "holier" or more "divine" than the other. Sacrament as well as Word ushers us into the "mystery of Godliness." We should not think of the Word as "mystical" and the sacrament as "mundane"; nor of the audible ("spiritual") message as superior to the visible and tangible ("physical") message. They are but two paths along the one Way.

God gave us the sacraments (as a "second" means of grace) not because his Word (as the "first" means of grace) is insufficient or unreliable or lacking in clarity and power. Our need for the visible and tangible elements of the sacraments is not a reflection upon God's Word, but upon our slowness of heart to believe. They are aids to help us better understand the full counsel of God. In them God condescends doubly to our dullness and weakness of mind. In view of our *untrustworthiness,* God underscores the *trustworthiness* of his Word in the symbols of the sacraments. In the sacramental elements He declares in unmistakable language: You can count on Me!

In our doubts and temptations we often turn to criticizing the Word. It's too hard to understand! It's too good to be true! To put an end to all contradiction, to affirm once-for-all the fullness of his grace in a clear-cut program of audio-visual instruction, God in the sacraments employs sign language to place his stamp of approval forever upon the promises of his Word.

10. Explain in what sense the effectiveness of both Word and sacrament depend upon the work of the Holy Spirit.

11. Why is the sacrament without the Word "magic"?

12. What do you think about the present trends in Roman Catholicism and Protestantism on this matter?

13. Are the sacraments "holier" than the Word? vice versa?

14. How should Word and sacrament be combined in our worship services?

15. How do the sacraments help us in our weakness?

Christian Baptism ────⬤25⬤────

Romans 6:1-11

Background to Baptism

Even if your parents were as poor as a church mouse, if in their arms you received the sign and seal of baptism, then you are fabulously rich! Not that the water was holy or costly. Not that the minister possessed some King Midas touch. Not that the congregation lavished its gifts upon you. Rather, in your baptism God made visible and tangible and audible for you the biblical truth: "Ye know the grace of our Lord Jesus Christ, that, though he was rich, yet for your sakes he became poor, that ye through his poverty might become rich" (II Cor. 8:9).

Baptism is an audio-visual version of the Good News. It is deeply embedded in the subsoil of the entire Bible. The roots of Christian baptism go back to the Old Testament sacrament of circumcision. Other peoples besides the Hebrews practiced circumcision. But for Abraham and his seed God instituted circumcision as a sacramental sign to seal his covenant with his elect people. The outward sign, however, was not an automatic guarantee. It was the circumcision of the heart that counted. Therefore "they are not all Israel, that are of Israel" (Rom. 9:6). Sacraments must always be embraced in faith, a faith that stands upon the ground of God's Word, the word of promise which in the Old Testament pointed forward to its fulfillment in our baptism through Christ.

For life in the Christian community Christ transformed circumcision into baptism. Note the words of the Baptismal Form, "Since then baptism has come in the place of circumcision (Col. 2:11-13)." But when Christ prescribed baptism in the Great Commission about A.D. 30, He was not introducing a previously unheard-of practice. Among both the Palestinian Jews and the dispersed Jews it was customary to baptize Gentiles who wished to accept the Jewish religion, short of being circumcised. For such so-called "God-fearers" (Acts 13:16; Luke 7:2-5) baptism was a kind of halfway-house initiation rite into the Jewish synagogue. They could worship and mingle with full-fledged Jews, but were not quite "members in full communion" of the Jewish community.

1. What riches, blessings, and advantages does baptism grant to Christians?
2. Explain how the element of **water** in baptism signifies and seals the saving grace of God through the **blood** of Christ.
3. What is the difference between Old Testament circumcision and New Testament baptism?
4. What is the difference between Christian baptism of its converts and Jewish baptism of its proselytes?

Prelude to Passion

From the Dead Sea Scrolls we learn that daily "baptisms" were an important part of the life of the Qumran community, a holiness sect living along the shoreline of the Dead Sea southeast of Jerusalem. Their water-baths were, however, quite unique. They were not once-for-all, but repeated. These lustrations were not initiation rites, but tokens of good standing in an elite society. They were not signs of conversion, but of on-going purification.

Some have argued that John the Baptist borrowed his "baptism of repentance" (Mark 1:4; Luke 3:3) from these Covenanters. There are, however, striking differences. To mention just one point: Qumran "baptisms" were clannish, whereas John challenged the whole nation by his call to repentance, confirmed by public baptisms down at the Jordan. By his entire ministry, preaching and baptizing, John was forging a redemptive link not between the Dead Sea Scrolls and the New Testament, but between the Old Testament and New Testament. John's *water*-baptism was a preparation for the coming *Spirit*-baptism (Matt. 3:11; Mark 1:8; Luke 3:16). The kingdom was coming just around the corner! John was its herald. His baptism was the baptism of the coming Spirit. Still there was a "not yet" dimension in John's ministry, something that fell short of the full reality. There was something of the "old" still mixed with the "new" (cf. Acts 19:1-7).

Crisis entered the life of the Baptist when Jesus confronted
him with the demand to be baptized. Baptize Christ? The baptism of repentance unto remission of sins! Preposterous! I need
it, not You! Impossible! But the impossible had to become
possible, even real, so that Christ could take the place of his
people, Jews and Gentiles alike. The Lord became a serf
to fulfill the law for us. So He plunged himself beneath the
filth-laden stream (the Jordan was a muddy, dirty river, cf.
II Kings 5:12) of human iniquity. At that moment *water*-
baptism and *Spirit*-baptism were united, the Spirit descending
upon the water-soaked Son as the Father voiced his approval
from heaven.

6. Explain how God in the case of baptism, as also in the case
   of circumcision and the Lord's Supper, that is, in all the
   sacraments, takes elements that belong to common human
   practice and consecrates them to sacramental usage.
7. What role did "water baptisms" play in the Qumran community?
8. Do you think it possible that John the Baptist or Jesus was
   somehow related to this community?
9. What was the importance of Christ's baptism for his work of
   redemption?
10 What is the relation between water-baptism and Spirit-bap-
   tism in the New Testament? Is this teaching a good ground
   for the Pentecostal doctrine of baptism by the Spirit as a
   "second blessing" for advanced Christians?

The Christian's Comfort

After Christ's blood-bath on the cross, which gives meaning
to our water-bath, the resurrected Lord pushed the program of
salvation forward by sending out his apostles to lay the
foundations of the church with this command: "Go ye therefore, and make disciples of all the nations, *baptizing* them into
the name of the Father and of the Son and of the Holy Spirit"
(Matt. 28:19). The basis for Christian baptism is therefore
obedience to Christ's command. In his Gospel Mandate preaching and baptizing, Word and sacrament, go hand in hand. As
an advance over John's baptism, Christ adds this new dimension: baptize into the name of (into the sphere of authority
of, into allegiance to) the triune God (cf. Matt. 28:19, 20).

The combination of water and the trinitarian formula is now the permanent test of a truly Christian baptism.

Paul, the "theologian" of the New Testament, spells out more fully the meaning of baptism. It means dying and rising with Christ (Rom. 6:4) and putting on Christ (Gal. 3:27). It is a cleansing bath (Titus 3:5). Baptism is not merely a *symbol* of a regenerate life (Zwinglianism). Nor is it the mysterious *cause* of the new life (Roman Catholicism). It is rather a *representation* (as a means of grace, as a sign and seal) of our participation in Good Friday and Easter. It confirms God's work *for us,* by justification, in the forgiveness of sin. It confirms God's work *in* us, by sanctification, in daily conversion. Baptism is the reassurance of what we *are* in Christ, and at the same time an exhortation increasingly to *become* what we are. It is the unshakable cornerstone of our hope, a ceaseless reminder of the awful reality of our *sin,* of the incalculable gift of *salvation,* and of the insistent call to *service.*

11. Can the parents of wayward children plead upon the baptismal promise?

12. Does every child born in the world have the "right" of baptism?

13. What should our attitude be to modernistic churches that baptize into the name of faith, hope, and love?

Covenant Children

What about children? Shall we exclude infants because they are incapable of an act of faith? Were they excluded in the old covenant? If the Old Testament embraced children together with their parents in the one people of God, why should we expect less in the New Testament? We look there in vain for any intimation that children have no place in the covenant. Taking seriously the unity of the Old and New Testaments we discover God's natural, organic way of working with men redemptively within the context of the familial and congregational ties that He has established in life (Gen. 12:3; Acts 2:39).

God does not deal with us atomistically, as isolated individuals, but as fathers and mothers, as husbands and wives, together with our children (cf. I Cor. 7:14). Creation and re-creation cannot be divorced. Redemption does not find its *power,* but it does find its *structure* in creation. For both are of God. He therefore incorporates children with their parents in both his judgment and his deliverance (Luke 23:28, 29). For together they belong to his covenant, his church, his kingdom.

The fact that there are no specific cases of infant baptism recorded in the Bible argues as much for it as against it. In the light of the wholeness of the Bible the burden of proof would seem to rest with those who reject infant baptism. The preoccupation of the young church with evangelism and missions may well explain the New Testament's silence on this point. Yet in the several known cases of household baptisms it would seem likely that some children were included (Acts 16:15, 33; 18:8; I Cor. 1:16).

14. Should we accept as valid the baptism of other churches?

15. How important do you think the question is of the **mode** of baptism (immersion vs. sprinkling)?

16. What do you think of the biblical case for infant baptism?

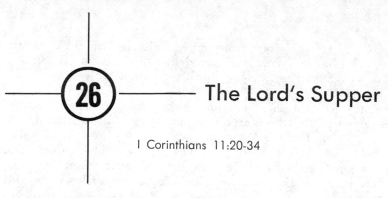

26 — The Lord's Supper

I Corinthians 11:20-34

Looking Backward and Forward

The Lord's Supper traces its *right* of existence and its *reason* for existence directly to its institution as a sacrament by Christ in the Upper Room on the evening of his betrayal. It constitutes a sovereign gift and command by the Lord to his disciples in every age. We have inherited five records of this charter of Christian reaffirmation and reassurance in the writings of Matthew, Mark, Luke, John, and Paul. Each writer casts a somewhat different light on this mystery. Yet altogether their united witness leaves us with a clear picture.

The long road of redemptive history reached a decisive turning-point when Christ as the Host reclined at the head of the table. In that meal, which was a sacramental *review* of the past and *preview* of the future, Christ symbolically interpreted the meaning of his cross in advance. Really it was a reinterpretation, for the Lord's Supper is a Christological updating of the age-old Passover. It was a sacramental transition, the great exchange, in which the Old and the New were finally bridged. For two meals were crowded into that one banquet, with the Passover as the appetizer and the Lord's Supper as the main course. The Passover was the preliminary and the Supper the feature event. It was the *last* Israelite meal and the *first* Christian feast.

Israel's annual Passover had a *backward* look, rehearsing God's mighty act of redemption in saving his people from the house of bondage. It was their unforgettable charter of liberation. Succeeding generations marked their calendar from that crucial event in the history of revelation, gathering momentum on its way to the fullness of the times.

But the Passover had built into it also a *forward* look. It was a promise and expectation of more to come. In its re-membrance of what had *already* happened there was also an outlook upon a reality not yet fully accomplished. The broiled lamb and unleavened bread contained something tentative, promissory, unfulfilled, predictive. Within this biblical tension between the *past* and the *future* the Old Testament believer celebrated the great feast of forgiveness.

Similarly, the New Testament sacrament of sacrifice is also an *interim* feast. It is caught in the high tension line between the first Advent and the re-Advent. As Paul puts it, "Do this in *remembrance* of me . . . *until he come again.*" Remembrance *and* expectation! At this Supper we cast our glances back across our shoulders to what has happened at Calvary, when the suf-fering Servant cried out, "It is finished!" Christ's once-for-all finished work is the fulfillment of the "not yet" Messianic hopes of the ancient Simeons who were looking forward to the con-solation of Israel. And today it is the pillar and ground upon which the church rests. The kingdom has in principle come! Victory is assured.

But we also look forward to the kingdom *yet to come* in all its perfection. We live anew as Christians in the dynamic tension between a redemptive work *already* accomplished and *not yet* perfected. The table of the Lord has an open end, a window that opens on the future. Peering through it we catch a glimpse of the time when this Supper will make way for the everlasting Marriage Feast of the Lamb. Recall Christ's words, "I will not drink of the fruit of the vine again until I drink it with you anew in the kingdom of my Father."

We therefore break the bread and pour out the wine between D-day and V-day — D-day, the day of God's great *decision* on Golgotha; V-day, the day of Christ's glorious *victory* when He shall be all in all. At the table, therefore, we look both back-ward and forward. God's *past* and his *future* define our pres-ent, teaching us through these signs and seals to lift up our hearts on high where Christ Jesus is, seated at the Father's right hand.

1. Try to uncover something of the unity and diversity in the five accounts of the first Lord's Supper.

2. Show how the Old and the New met together in the Upper Room.

3. Is it right to speak of the **first** Lord's Supper as "The **Last** Supper," as Leonardo da Vinci's famous painting is entitled?

4. Do you think that in our communion services "the past is too much with us"?

5. How do Paul's words, "Let Christ dwell in you **by faith**," apply to our partaking of the Lord's Supper?

6. In what sense is the Lord's Supper an **interim** feast?

Worthy Partakers

Christians seem sometimes to regard Holy Communion as an extra special religious experience. The pulpit may be "the holy place," but the table is "the holy of holies." As pilgrims we trudge along through the barren wildernesses of life. But a few times a year we reach a higher plateau, an oasis in the desert, mountaintop experiences that lift us out of the valleys of the shadow of death up to higher ground.

Therefore some Christians plead for more frequent celebration of Communion in order to inhale this exhilarating mountain air more fully. The more of such "retreats" the better! Others argue that since the Supper is so extraordinarily sacred, we should celebrate it sparingly, lest it become commonplace.

It is not, however, the *reasons* men give, but the *meaning* God places in the sacrament that decides the questions of frequency and worthy participation. The certainty of the sacrament lies not in our eating and drinking, nor in our faith, but in the fact that we receive these elements out of the hand of the Lord himself. As baptism represents our initiation into the Christian community, so the Lord's Supper represents our ongoing fellowship therein. Receiving these symbols believingly is our "amen" upon the promises of God given in the sprinkled water. It is a confession of our faith before God and the world, but at the same time an expression of our sense of weakness and need for renewal. It is a reaffirmation of the gospel of reconciliation in the Word, offering us no more and no less and nothing else than the one message of God's grace, though in a different way.

Because of the close interconnection and correlation between the sacrament and the Word and faith, Calvin was in favor of very frequent, even weekly, partaking of the bread and the

wine. Quarterly celebration, however, became the general practice in Reformed circles, but only as a minimum.

Yet, whether weekly, or monthly, or bimonthly, or quarterly,
we desecrate the sacrament if we push it into some hole-in-the-
corner, isolated from the rest of Christian living, whether out of
deference to it as a super-mystery, or disparagement of it as
an irregularity to be endured. It must stand squarely in the
middle of the main stream of the Christian life. It is our staff
of life, our food and drink unto eternal life, and life here
and now.

Paul found it necessary in Corinth, his ecclesiastical problem
child, to emphasize strongly worthy participation. Our *worthiness* depends basically on a personal sense of *unworthiness.*
Without the sincere prayer, "Lord, I believe; help thou my
unbelief," we stymie this sacramental means of grace. Our
mouths may then move in unison with the congregation, but
the Spirit withholds his blessing. For a Judas and a Simon the
Sorcerer break faith with Christ and disrupt the fellowship of
the saints.

7. How can we put our weeks of preparation to best use?
8. How frequently do you think we should celebrate the Supper?
9. What does Paul mean by "eating and drinking judgment unto
   ourselves, if we discern not the body"?

Communion or Controversy?

It is a strange and tragic thing that this sacrament of
Christian communion has occasioned so much theological controversy. The conflicts center most specifically around the
question of the *real presence* of Christ in the sacrament.

Spiritualists, on the one hand, tend to *downgrade* the sacrament as too earthly and debasing. Roman Catholicism, on the
other hand, upholds the theory of *transubstantiation,* the idea
that the priestly act of consecration actually changes the essence of the bread and wine into the body and blood of
Christ, even though the accidental features of sight, touch, and
taste remain the same. Lutheranism, reacting to both of these
views, defends *consubstantiation,* teaching that Christ's body and
blood are physically present in, under, and with the bread
and the wine. Zwinglianism, the forerunner of many modern

liberal views of the sacrament, regards the sacrament merely as a *memorial* that we Christians erect in honor to Christ. Amid this theological confusion, Calvin confessed the *real spiritual presence of Christ.* The Supper is both symbol and reality. In it we receive not only Christ's sacramental *gifts,* but in them we receive the seal of our fellowship with the *Giver* himself. Through his Spirit and by a living faith we are united with him in his death and resurrection. All that He *is* and all that He *has* becomes ours in eating and drinking in remembrance of him until He comes again.

10. Is the Heidelberg Catechism justified in describing the Roman Catholic view of Christ's presence in the sacrament as an "accursed idolatry"?

11. Is our Reformed thinking and practice on the Lord's Supper drifting in a Zwinglian direction?

12. Should we maintain close communion? or open communion?

13. What does it mean that a Christian should come to the age of discretion before partaking of the Lord's Supper?

Offices in the Church ———(**27**)———

I Peter 5:1-11

The Biblical Idea of Office

In God's grand plan for creation our lives are made up of various *spheres* of activity. We live and move and have our being within such spheres as home life, education, church, civil government, daily vocations, recreation, and so on. All these spheres are anchored in divinely given laws for human life. God himself is supremely sovereign over all of life. He exercises his sovereign rule through the power and light of his Word. Under its Maker, each sphere in life has a sovereignty of its own, given by God and answerable to God. These rights and duties of each sphere must be honored and upheld as divinely given, inalienable, and inviolable ordinances. Thus, under God, the home within the precincts of its own conscience must answer the question of planned parenthood. Thus, the school, under God, must have freedom from all outside interference to decide in principle and practice its own philosophy of education. Thus, too, under God, Scripture directs us to insist on the separation of church and state.

Functioning within each sphere in life, man takes his place as a divinely appointed *officer*. Man was created as prophet, priest, and king. We are therefore obliged to exercise our triple office in every sphere of life: as parents in the home, as teachers or society members in the school, as leaders or followers in the church, as citizens or councilmen in government, as laborers in the union. All of this with a view to crowning Christ as Lord of all.

There are three main aspects to the biblical idea of office. First, there is a sovereign *authority* that God delegates to men in their various callings in life. We have no natural rights. Nought have we gotten but what we have received. Hence, in reply to Pilate's claim, "Don't you know that I have the power [authority, right] to release you?" Christ drove the point home by replying, "You would have no power at all, if it were not given to you from above" (John 19:11). This is true for every office we hold in every sphere in life.

Second, for the exercise of our sovereign authority, subservient only to the supreme sovereignty of God, we are *responsible* to the God who gave it. Someday, somehow, God will call upon us to give an account of our stewardship. Such a sense of responsibility to God lends character and purpose to Christian living: responsibility in the exercise of parental authority in the home, responsibility in the exercise of academic freedom in the school, responsibility in the exercise of synodical-classical-consistorial authority in the church.

Third, we must use this responsible authority in such a way as to be *serviceable* to those who share with us in the blessings of each sphere in life. As husbands, for example, we are obliged to serve our wives and children in love. As teachers, to educate our students well and thus to serve the community for whose benefit they are being trained. As citizens, to serve the best interests of the kingdom of God in today's society. As ministers, to serve the congregations over which we are placed as undershepherds.

1. On the basis of Genesis 1:27-31, how would you define the office of husband and wife (Adam and Eve) in the home? How does man exercise his God-given office in the pursuit of this cultural mandate?

2. How is the sovereignty of each sphere in life related to the coexisting sovereignty of other spheres and the supreme sovereignty of God?

3. Explain how the above three aspects of office (authority, responsibility, and serviceability) apply to the three special offices in the church.

Universal Office in the Church

We are accustomed to speaking of believers in general as *laymen*. This word has a pretty checkered career. The Bible speaks of God's people as the *laos*, the root word for laity. But after biblical times the word laity has become laden with less desirable meanings. Since medieval times, when it was used to distinguish the laity from the clergy, it has carried with it strong Roman Catholic overtones. The clergy was viewed as the *soul* of the church, the laity the *body;* the clergy the *teaching* church, the laity the *listening* church; the clergy *active,* the laity *passive.*

The Reformers broke through this traditional definition by insisting that *all* believers are members of the church in full communion. Every Christian is called to full-time kingdom service. Romish clericalism which reduces nonministerial church members to inactivity and expects laymen simply to "obey, pray, and pay," is a serious departure from scriptural teaching. Luther and Calvin, therefore, both proclaimed the freedom of all Christians to serve God without a guilty conscience in all the callings of life.

We would do well to coin a substitute for the word *laity,* or else free it of its traditional inferiority complex, or better still revive the original biblical meaning of *laos.*

The primary office in the church is not the special office of deacon, elder, or minister, but the universal office of every believer. This is the foundation that undergirds church life. The three special offices are but specializations on the triple office of all Christians, the prophetic, priestly, and kingly office being expressed in the minister, deacon, and elder. These special offices represent sovereign authorities bestowed by Christ, for the exercise of which those holding these special offices are responsible to the King of the church, in the exercise of which they are called to serve God's people. The special office must serve, not subdue, the general office.

4. How do you feel about the use of the words **layman** and **laity**?

5. How would you argue the case that all Christians are called to full-time kingdom service?

6. How can we prevent overbearing clericalism and encourage healthy lay activity?

7. How are the general and special offices in the church related to each other?

8. Does ecclesiastical authority belong to persons as **persons** or to persons in their **offices**?

Special Offices in the Church

In the early Christian church we see in operation the extra-ordinary office of apostle. The apostles were the avenues of divine revelation to the church through the New Testament writings. Thus they served as links between Christ and the Christian community. The basis for divine appointment to the office of apostle was the decisive fact of having been eye and ear witnesses to the life and death and resurrection of the Lord (Acts 1:21, 22). The office of apostle was therefore unique and exclusive. It died with the apostles themselves.

At this point Rome and the Reformation part ways. Roman Catholicism in its doctrine of apostolic succession teaches that the office of apostle lives on in the Roman hierarchy. Peter was the prince of the apostles, the first bishop of Rome, and thus the rock upon which the papacy rests.

The Reformers rejected this whole idea of the hierarchy. Christ, through the extraordinary office of the apostles, provided for the special offices of ministers, elders, and deacons in the church. But among these offices there is a basic unity and equality. As the newly revised Church Order puts it: "These offices differ from each other only in mandate and task, not in dignity and honor."

Often a false spirit of democracy stands in the way of rightful recognition of and respect for these special offices. In those who faithfully serve these offices, Christ himself comes to us. Therefore we should gladly receive the services which the church offers us through these special offices as coming not from neighbor John Smith, but elder John Smith, a servant of the Master.

The newly revised Church Order defines the work of the special officers as follows:

"The task of the *minister* is to preach the Word, administer the sacraments, conduct public worship services, and catechize the youth in order that the church may be built and unbelievers won for Christ."

"The *elders,* with the minister, shall have supervision over the congregation and their fellow office-bearers, exercising admonition and discipline and seeing to it that everything is done decently and in good order. They shall, with the minister, exercise pastoral care over the congregation, and engage in and promote the work of evangelism."

"The task of the *deacons* is to administer Christian mercy toward those who are in need, first of all toward those of the household of faith, but also toward the needy in general. In executing this task they shall diligently collect, administer, and distribute monies and other gifts, and shall serve the distressed with counsel and assistance. They shall enable the needy under their care to make use of Christian institutions of mercy. They shall confer and cooperate with diaconates of neighboring churches when this is desirable for the proper performance of their task. They may also seek mutual understandings with other agencies in their community which are caring for the needy, so that the gifts may be distributed properly."

9. By what right does Paul claim to be an apostle?

10. Does Matthew 16:18 support the Roman Catholic doctrine of apostolic succession and the primacy of Peter?

11. Does a false democratic spirit sometimes stand in our way in honoring the authority of the special offices?

12. Should we have bishops in our church?

13. Is the current prosperity and extension of social security under-cutting the work of the diaconate and robbing the church of its ministry of mercy?

14. Are we loading down our ministers with administrative duties, our elders with business transactions, and our deacons with high finance to the point where their energies are being diverted from their central tasks?

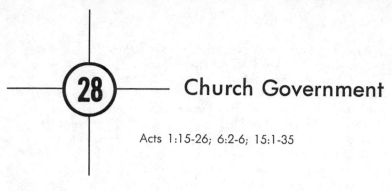

Church Government

Acts 1:15-26; 6:2-6; 15:1-35

Biblical Guidelines

The "roaring twenties" witnessed a classic example of modern church union. In 1925 the United Church of Canada began to advertise itself as "the uniting church" as a result of the organizational reunion of all Methodist and Congregational churches and most Presbyterian churches across the dominion. This ecumenical break-through created many difficulties, of course — confessional, liturgical, historical, and traditional difficulties. Also difficulties in the area of church government. After all, how could three denominations with three different patterns of church polity — episcopalian, independent, and presbyterian — expect to live together as one happy family under a single ecclesiastical roof?

Behind this question, however, looms the larger and more basic question, whether the Bible lays any specific foundations for church government. Answering this question, some claim too much, others too little. Some *literalists* insist that Scripture explicitly prescribes a detailed blueprint for church polity after the fashion of Robert's *Rules of Order*. Some *historicists* argue that Scripture is silent on these matters, and that therefore every church is free to draft its own constitution in accordance with practical circumstances.

It must be granted that we cannot read back completely any one of our present systems of church government into the life of the apostolic age. Times change, and the church must adjust its practices to meet the shifting scenes of modern society. Still, the New Testament (especially The Acts and the epistles) quite unmistakably provides central directives for the life of the church today. In these apostolic records we discover a general framework and some fundamental guidelines. The

134

Master has not left his servants without a charter in conducting ecclesiastical business in an ecclesiastical way. The ongoing acts of Christ through the apostles under the Spirit have a permanent normative value.

With this kind of backing the early church was compelled to work out answers to unprecedented problems. It had no Index to the *Acts of Synod* to refer to in deciding issues. But gradually a pattern developed. Steadily the pieces began to fall more clearly into place. Out of their united action two basic principles for church order emerge for our instruction. *First,* we see the living fellowship of the one, holy catholic church worshiping and witnessing and working as the people of God in the world. Such unity condemns all sectarianism, independentism, and undenominationalism. It lays the groundwork upon which the church stands in meeting jointly for concerted action in its major assemblies and ecumenical councils. No congregation is self-sufficient (I Cor. 14:36). The sovereign home rule of each local church must be exercised within the framework of Christian catholicity, thus maintaining the identity of the local church and expressing its universality.

Second, each local congregation is an unabridged version of the universal church, possessing the fullness of Christ's gifts and powers and Spirit. Such local sovereignty and full-fledged representation is an indictment of all top-heavy hierarchical church rule and synodical tyranny and overbearing boardism and concentration of church political power in highly centralized steering committees.

These are biblical principles that undergird the Presbyterian-Reformed type of church government.

1. Is agreement on church polity important for united church life?
2. How do the **structures** of the church influence the **spirit** in the church?
3. Show how the Jerusalem Conference (Acts 15) reflects the interaction of the local church and the church universal.
4. What are the features of the congregational-independent form of church government? the hierarchical-episcopalian form of church government?
5. Do you think the recent action of the Second Vatican Council in establishing a college of bishops to assist the pope in church rule will make the Roman Catholic Church more "presbyterian"?

Local Church

The death of the apostles did not leave the church with an apostolic vacuum. The one apostolic office became diversified in the many general and special offices in the church. Thus the Christological byproducts of the apostles accrued to the body through the gifts of the Spirit. The church is still apostolic. With Pentecost the church came of age. Therefore no man may "play pope" in the church. Therefore also no consistory may "go its own way," acting as "a law unto itself." Acts 1 and 6 exemplify the kind of interaction that should prevail between the apostolic *general* office and the apostolic *special* office in the church. The man in the pew must exercise his right and duty of approbation as he listens to sermons, thus placing his "Amen" upon the Word proclaimed. In congregational meetings the members of the church both elect and pass judgment upon their office-bearers, and also submit themselves to the rule of their undershepherds.

Yet, the church is not a democratic society. The congregation must honor the apostolic authority that the King of the church delegates to those invested in special office. Thus the consistory (session) becomes the basic unit upon which church government rests. It authorizes the minister to preach the Word. It calls the congregation together at stated times for worship. After congregational balloting, the consistory takes the decisive step in calling a minister. The consistory takes leadership in presenting matters for congregational action. It is the responsible ruling body in the church. It seeks representation in the major assemblies and delegates certain powers to these gatherings. See Acts 15:2; I Corinthians 16:3; and II Corinthians 8:19.

6. How do Acts 1 and 6 exemplify the interaction of the **special** and **general** offices in the church in arriving at decisions? Point out the **theocratic** element in both cases.

7. Should the consistory consult the congregation in preparing to call a minister?

8. When should consistories seek the advice of neighboring churches and the classis?

Major Assemblies

The ruling structures of the church are manifested specifically and permanently in the local churches. But from time to time the local church embraces fellow churches in a broader (not higher!) fellowship at major assemblies — classes (presbyteries), regional synods, general synods, and ecumenical synods. These bodies have no permanent standing. They come into existence and go out of existence at the call of some local church acting for the churches unitedly. Therefore presbyterianism does not allow for bishops and archbishops exercising higher supervision, since it views the New Testament offices of *bishop* and *presbyter* as equivalent to the ruling elder of the local church (the minister also serving in governmental matters as an elder). See Acts 20:17, 28; Titus 1:5, 7; Philippians 1:1; I Timothy 3:1-8.

United in confession and church polity, these major assemblies transact whatever business pertains to the interest and welfare of the churches in general, plus matters that cannot be brought to a successful conclusion within the local church. Here is a forum for mutual counsel and supervision. Classes arrange for annual church visitation by classical delegates with the consistory of local churches. The major assemblies offer a court of appeal for persons who feel unjustly treated by their local churches. Here the churches unitedly admit candidates to the ministry of the church at large, though called to a local church. Here the churches seek in unison to discharge their common calling in missions and evangelism, in college and seminary education, and in the ministry of mercy to men in need.

Among the Reformed churches the broadest major assembly today is the Reformed Ecumenical Synod. By delegated authority, some forty churches around the world seek through this medium to express their catholicity. Questions of mutual concern appear on the agenda: the conflict between creationism and evolutionism, the race problem, and the nature and task of the church in our modern world.

By such interacting cooperation between local churches and the major assemblies, presbyterianism offers a system of checks and balances in church government which averts the extremes of both papal dominance and undisciplined democracy. Rather than rule in the hands of *one* or *all*, government in the hands of *many* is better than government in the hands of *few* (as Calvin held).

9. Do you think classical and synodical agendas are becoming too lengthy because of the failure of local churches to do their homework?

10. What biblical-theological reasons can you offer for checks and balances in church government?

11. Why is church visitation important?

The Coming of the Kingdom

Matthew 13

His Truth Is Marching On

"Seek ye first his kingdom . . ." (Matt. 6:33). In this royal command, Christ the Servant-King proclaims the central theme of the gospel. In the Bible, from Genesis to Revelation, we witness God's great kingdom-drama — the kingdom created, disrupted, reestablished, now advancing, and one day to be perfected. It began as a Garden. It ends as the New Jerusalem. The Christian church here and now plays a leading role in the program of this coming kingdom. The Lord is our Shepherd, and we, the sheep of his flock, are the servants in his kingdom.

God is Lord of general revelation and special revelation. He is Ruler in the order of creation and in the order of redemption. All history is the unfolding of his kingdom plan. Therefore Christians in every age acknowledge the sovereignty of God in all of life, in home and school, in work and play, and everywhere along the way. The charter of the kingdom is the cross and the empty tomb. On this firm foundation God now exercises his sovereign grace and power through the kingly rule of Christ in judgment and redemption.

Yet repeatedly the cry goes up, "We have no king but Caesar!" The Caesars of nuclear stockpiles, of power politics, of union tyranny, of the almighty dollar, of status symbols, of hootenanny blasts, of Ivy League diplomas, of self-improvement programs, of religiosity.

In this rebellious world the King, his kingship, and his kingdom meet strong resistance. This is the gospel record. The Lord sends his servants, the prophets, to gather the fruits of his royal vineyard. But manhandled and mangled, they meet a stony death. At the peak of harvest-time he sends the Crown

Prince. But the evil husbandmen shout in chorus: We will not that this Man should rule over us! Away with him! Crucify him! The King came to his subjects, but they turned him down. Yet He who sits in the heavens laughed: laughter of derision at puny man's futile plot, laughter of delight at his redemptive mission accomplished.

Was Christ victim or victor? Listen: because Christ humbled himself and became obedient unto the death of the cross, therefore God has highly exalted him and given him the name above every name, that at the name of Jesus every knee should bow and every tongue confess that He is Lord to the glory of God the Father (Phil. 2:9-11).

1. In which ways can we see the unity of Christ's kingdom with the theocracy in the Old Testament?

2. What kinds of idols do men serve these days instead of Christ the King?

3. How do you explain the fact that there are such varied results upon the preaching of the Word of the kingdom (Matt. 13:1-23)?

The Cross and the Crown

In fulfilling his royal mandate Christ took all the Messianic titles of the Old Testament — the Star of Jacob, the Prince of Peace, the Lion of the Tribe of Judah, David's Son and David's Lord — and made them his own. He took the regal benediction, "a kingdom of priests and a holy nation," and transferred it from Israel to that new Christian community which had responded to his kingly call: "Follow me!"

Most of the Jews were offended at this King. Indeed, they wanted a king, a social reformer, a military champion, a Führer to beat down the hated Romans. An earthly empire. A Jewish nationalistic utopia. But the prophecy of a King who would come as a suffering Servant, meek and lowly, and riding on a donkey — of all things, not this! They had set their minds on a power kingdom, not a kingdom of righteousness.

Therefore the royal herald, John the Baptist, had to pave the way by proclaiming, "Repent, for the kingdom of heaven is at hand!" Behold his baptism! Baptism with fire for the rebels. Baptism with the Holy Spirit for the loyalists.

The Master was also the Minister (Matt. 20:28). He had to stoop to conquer. The great stumbling block! If only the Lord could avoid being a Servant. Peter blurted it out: "Nay, this shall never be unto thee!" But the way to the crown (Col. 1:15-20) was the way of the cross (Heb. 12:2). But once glorified, King Jesus affirmed his unlimited authority, conferred upon us an unlimited task, and assured us of his unlimited companionship (Matt. 28:18-20).

4. Why did the Jews react so strongly against the sign on the cross, "Jesus, the King of the Jews"?

5. Why does God allow the wheat and the tares (two antithetical kingdoms) to grow together in this world (Matt. 13:24-30, 36-43)?

6. From the Great Commission, what can we learn about the relationship between missions and the kingdom?

Past, Present, Future

Many Christians with premillennial views look upon the kingdom as an exclusively future reality, to which we can only look forward by watching and prayer. They contend that the design for kingdom living, as given in the Sermon on the Mount, is reserved for the time after Christ's return when He will reign upon the earth for a thousand years.

Others hold that Christ was cheated by death in his attempt to establish the kingdom in his day. When the King died, the kingdom died with him. The rules given in the Sermon on the Mount, it is said, were intended for the interim until the kingdom was to be established. But, the kingdom defeated, these rules no longer hold. The apostles, however, unwilling to quit, ushered in the church as a substitute for the lost kingdom.

On the latter view, the kingdom is *no longer* a reality. On the former view, it is *not yet* a reality. Neither one has a message for today, here and now. Historic Christianity replies in its joyful hymn:

> *The Lord is come . . . the Savior reigns,*
> *Let earth receive her King!*

Biblical faith throws its windows open both to the *past* (a finished work of redemption) and to the *future* (the kingdom perfected). The kingdom is here in *principle,* and is moving forward to its *consummation.* We live "between God's times," between D-day (decision day at Calvary) and V-day (victory day ahead). The conflict continues between the kingdom of light and the kingdom of darkness. But the outcome is *already* settled. The antichrist is fighting a losing battle. We are more than conquerors. There is a daily answer to the prayer, "Thy kingdom come!" Still, the best is *yet to come.* Here and now, our *present* duty must be defined within the biblical tension of the kingdom-come and the kingdom-to-come.

7. Is the kingdom past? or future? or past, future, and present?

8. How does the example of D-day and V-day help us understand the progress of the coming of the kingdom?

9. How does the parable of the Mustard Seed (Matt. 13:31, 32) apply to the coming of the kingdom today?

Christ Shall Have Dominion

The *kingdom* and the *church* are as closely interrelated as a *program* and the *people* involved in it. The church, as the people of God, is the population of the kingdom. There the fulfillment of the kingdom is eagerly expected. There the gifts and powers of the kingdom are displayed. There the impulse to Christian witness in every nook and cranny of life is generated, deepened, enriched. Worship is unto work, Sunday unto Monday, liturgy unto life, sermons unto service. For the sway of Christ's kingdom extends beyond the boundaries of the church.

As Abraham Kuyper put it, "There is not one square inch of all the universe of which Christ the Lord does not say, 'This is mine.'"

> *Christ shall have dominion over land and sea,*
> *Earth's remotest regions shall his empire be.*

The Christian must honor Christ's claim upon every area of life, and seek to press that claim wherever possible. The sovereignty of God and the kingship of Christ are counterparts. Every sphere of life falls under this royal rule: Christ the Head of our home, the Lord of our lands, the Director of our businesses, the Lawgiver of our unions, the Commander-in-chief of the body politic, the Superintendent of our schools at every level of education. In every sphere of life we are all called to be full-time kingdom workers. And every day counts for the coming of the kingdom of grace and glory.

10. What does the parable of the Leaven teach us about the way the kingdom works in the world (Matt. 13:33)?

11. How are the church and the kingdom interrelated?

12. How must we witness to the sovereignty of God and the king-ship of Christ in the spheres of life mentioned above?

30 — Signs of the Times

Matthew 24; II Thessalonians 2:1-11

The March of Time

Christ came in "the fulness of time." He spoke of this as "my day." On the way to the cross He frequently commented, "My hour is not yet come." During the passion week He announced, "In three days I will be delivered up." But He added the promise, "After three days I will rise again." The picture is clear. Christ is the Lord of history. Time is under his control.

Nowadays, however, many theologians are broadcasting the news that Christ was badly mistaken, seriously shortsighted in viewing the time of his return. He allegedly miscalculated future events. Thus He misled his disciples into thinking that his return was just around the corner, a few short years at the most.

Certainly He never left any doubt that the time leading up to his return would be laden with immediate imperative and pressing urgency. "Behold, I come quickly!"

Still, Christ's preview of the New Age allows for the passage of whatever time God allots for the building of his church and the coming of his kingdom. He speaks, for example, of the future destruction of Jerusalem, the progressive evangelizing of the nations, the growth of the tiny mustard seed into a large tree, and the on-going leavening of the lump. This all suggests time for the gospel program to run its full course.

Some regard the cross as the end of a good beginning for Christ. In reality, however, with his redemptive mission accomplished, all of time since then is the beginning of the End Time. We have no reason to look for new saving acts of God until the Day of the Lord finally breaks. Every day between D-day and V-day belongs to the "last days."

But Christ has not given us a timetable by which to date his return. The calendar of the New Age hangs in heaven, not on earth. In his Servant role Christ reminds us that only the Father knows the day and the hour. All guesswork is vetoed in advance. Any day could be the day, whether in the first century or the twentieth. His coming is always at hand. This is our Lord's language. This was the eager faith of early Christians. This hope is still alive today. Or is it? Maranatha!

Yet, what about the prolonged "delay"? Already in his day Peter had to endure the derision of complacent skeptics, who discredited the Christians' forward- and upward-looking expectation with their taunts about all things being ever the same. Where are the signs of his approaching return (II Peter 3:3, 4)? Now 1900 years have elapsed. And who knows, perhaps God has another thousand years in store for his world. Even then, Christian faith can absorb this watching and waiting and working.

The most sobering sign of these times is the reality of the intermediate state between death and resurrection. Sin still pays its wages in death. We all move toward that inescapable exit, the last enemy, that unnatural encounter. But Christ's victory means the death of death. Its sting is healed. The grave was buried with Christ. There is light in the darkness, a smile through the tears. And comfort, and hope, and glory. Whether we live or whether we die, we are the Lord's — we, the whole "we," our real self. Yet a corpse is laid to rest.

Here the Bible draws the curtain. We are allowed just a distant glimpse into the life beyond this life. The stand we take here and now decides our status over there, whether hell or heaven, utter alienation or communion forever. For believers the intermediate state brings with it the greatest glory possible for disembodied men. Blessed are the dead who die in the Lord. The present glory of those who have fallen asleep in the Lord is the sure sign (and promise and pledge) of greater glory still to come when Christ returns in his resurrection power.

1. Was Christ mistaken about the time of his return?
2. Was the expectation of the early Christians shortsighted?
3. In what sense does every day since Christ's time belong to the "last days"?

4. How can we best describe the light and shadow side of death for the believer?

5. How much does the Bible reveal about life in the intermediate state?

6. Is there any reason to think of the intermediate state as a soul-sleep or an unconscious existence?

7. Does Scripture offer any hope of a "second chance" after this life?

Signs along the Way

Meanwhile, Scripture focuses our attention upon at least three signals heralding the Day of days.

First, there is the worldwide preaching of the gospel (Matt. 24:14). It started with Pentecost. Its end is hidden from view. When the divinely appointed purpose of universal evangelization will have reached its fulfillment, we cannot say. It is ours to help hasten that day by faithful obedience to the Great Commission.

The *second* signal is the persisting turmoil of mankind awaiting the New Order and the groaning of all creation awaiting its final redemption (Rom. 8:22, 23). Perhaps the most telling signal is this, that the signs are hung out like brilliantly lit neon billboards, but men hurry by, oblivious to it all. Seeing, they see not!

Third, the Bible foretells the appearance of "the man of sin" (II Thess. 2:8-10) as the forerunner of Christ's re-advent. Antichrists and antichristian powers are legion (I John 2:18, 22). But in the end, apparently everything antichristian will head up in one great deceiver. An antichristian boycott! Inquisition! Terror on the earth! Will even the elect fall? But the time will be shortened.

In this context Paul speaks of a "restraint" and a "restrainer," presently checking the outburst of evil in the world, but later to be withdrawn. Then, as time runs out on our world, we will witness for the first time in all history the uninhibited potentials of total depravity unrestrained by common grace. What if government erodes, and conscience degenerates, and law and order disappear, and public opinion dies as a stabilizing factor in society? Then our cursory prayer may become a fervent plea: "Come, Lord Jesus, come quickly!"

8. Is there any way of knowing how close we are to a fulfillment of the Great Commission?
9. Do the troubles of our times serve to turn men's hearts to the great Day?
10. What picture does the Bible present of the "man of sin"?
11. Is it thinkable that the withdrawal of the restraining effects of common grace may pave the way for the great tribulations preceding Christ's return?

Getting Ready

As the year 1000 dawned, people were sure they saw the handwriting on the wall. But, once past, their nervous, fingernail-biting anxiety turned to reveling. Others fixed the date anew, 1914. They gave up their jobs, sold their property (precisely the wrong way to get ready!); they put on white robes and sat on roofs to watch and wait. When the day passed, without catastrophe, they recalculated, and then finally concluded that the kingdom had indeed broken through that day, but invisibly.

Generally, however, men breathe a spirit of quite total indifference. For the "last days" will be like the days of Noah and Lot, with men pursuing the order of the day, eating and drinking, marrying and working and playing — all good gifts, but received in blindness to the Giver. A secular society will prevail — a society where God doesn't count. For while men are getting better at predicting the weather (Matt. 16:1-3), they are becoming illiterates in reading the signs of the times.

Still, the signs are there for all to see. Perhaps not so much in spectacular events as in the "normal" trends of history. For example: forty-four wars in the past two decades, research labs replacing churches, weekends for leisure instead of Sundays for worship.

The signs are out: the Bridegroom's reminders to his bride that He has not forgotten their appointed date!

12. What is wrong with setting dates for Christ's return?
13. Do you think the final stages of history will be characterized by usual or unusual events?
14. What are Christians called to do in preparing for Christ's return?

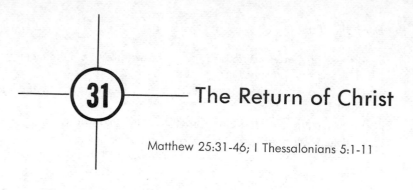

The Return of Christ

Matthew 25:31-46; I Thessalonians 5:1-11

Parousia

Each year we stop, look, and listen to the redemptive message of the series of red-letter days on our church calendar — such holidays as Christmas, Good Friday, Easter, Ascension, and Pentecost. All of these are days of remembrance, pointing to a 1900-year-old past, calling upon us to cast our glances back across our shoulders to what has already happened, once and for all.

But what about the future? Should the church commemorate in advance the one great act of God in history still to come? A few years ago the general assembly of a church was asked to designate a *Parousia* Sunday, one day annually to focus the church's faith on the hope of Christ's return (which is what the New Testament word *parousia* means). That general assembly decided, however, that such a forward-looking faith is not something for a single Sunday, but for every Sunday. This eschatological hope in gospel preaching and in gospel living should give a slant to every day in our lives. Always keep your windows open to the second coming of the Lord.

One wonders, however, whether Paul's *Maranatha* (I Cor. 16:22) is a very active part of our vocabulary these days. A generation or two ago, it seems, this outstretched, tiptoed expectation was more alive in some circles than it is today. In retrospect, hardly a Sunday went by without the congregational prayer closing on the climactic note, "Come, Lord Jesus, come quickly!" (As a boy I used to react: "Okay, but not too quickly, 'cause I've got a little living to do yet!")

Early Christians saluted each other on the streets with the greeting: "He is risen!" Now that the world has spent nearly two thousand years creating new crises upon the ruins of old ones — world wars, depressions, poverty, concentration camps, population explosions, space races, and hanging over it all the threat of "the bomb" — perhaps the time is ripe for Christians to greet each other with the reminder: "He is coming again!"

Sunday by Sunday, of course, we mouth the confession, "from whence He shall come again to judge the living and the dead." But does that faith really change anything in our lives? The conveniences of an affluent economy and the securities of a "Great Society" leave many of us with the illusion that God's "New Order" is now at last almost within our grasp, if only. . . .

The little old lady in the Amsterdam trolley was on the right track. As she mounted the platform laboriously the conductor lent her a hand and remarked, "Lady, you've seen your best days too." To which she replied, with a twinkle in her eye, "No, sir, my best days are still coming!"

1. Do you agree that the general assembly referred to above made the right decision?

2. Do you think our present social and economic conditions affect our outlook upon Christ's second coming?

3. Is man capable of bringing the world to an end by his own destructive powers?

4. Is man capable of ushering in the "New Order" as the result of his cultural achievements?

Maranatha

The second coming of Christ is an article of the Christian faith. It is not something we can "prove" with scientific evidence. What "proofs" could we possibly use? A boy, for example, cannot *prove* that his dad loves him. The skeptic might argue that his father's display of goodness was just sham or pretense. Yet way down deep in his heart the boy *knows* (though he cannot "prove" it) beyond the shadow of the slightest doubt that his father's love is real. Similarly, the Christian, with an appeal to Scripture, stakes his whole future on the reality of Christ's return. Slightly amended, he sings the children's hymn:

> *Jesus is coming, this I know,*
> *For the Bible tells me so.*

Scripture lays a double foundation beneath this hope. *First,* turning back to what Christ has already done for us, we turn to face his final act in the drama of redemption with confidence. He will return in judgment. But for the believer, God's judgment has already been taken care of at the cross. If God loved us then, while we were enemies, He will love us still when Christ returns to separate the wheat from the tares (Acts 17:30-31; Rom. 5:8-10). *Second,* turning back to Christ's clear promise of the impending V-day, we can turn to the Day of the Lord and trade anxiety for anticipation. The Master reassures his disciples, "I go to prepare a place for you. . . . I come again, and will receive you unto myself; that where I am, there ye may be also" (John 14:2-3).

There are at least three features of the second coming of Christ that are highlighted in Scripture. *First,* it will be sudden and unexpected. As lightning streaks from horizon to horizon (Luke 17:24), so divine judgment will instantaneously cut across all the lines of human history. As thieves break in at the most untimely and inconvenient hours, so Christ's return will take men by surprise (II Peter 3:10). It will strike so swiftly as to sweep men off their feet — "in the twinkling of an eye" (I Cor. 15:52). *Second,* "that great and notable day" will dawn with an unmistakable clarity. Therefore, if at any time people should say, "Lo, He is here!" or "Lo, there!" don't bother to check it out. Forget it, and get on with your calling. Disregard all such false alarms. For the kingdom will not come "with observation" (Luke 17:20-21), that is, it will not take a trained eye to detect it. When it happens, you will know it — and good! *Third,* Christ's coming will carry in it a universal sweep. It will introduce a cosmic renovation (Rom. 8:20-23). All men, the sheep and the goats, the great and the small, even those who pierced him, will encounter Christ as Judge (Matt. 25:32; Mark 13:27; Phil. 2:10-11; Rev. 1:7).

5. Upon what basis does our faith in Christ's second coming rest?

6. Do you know of any "false alarms" that men have sounded to announce the arrival of the Day of the Lord?

7. Can you explain the difference between premillennialism, postmillennialism, and amillennialism? Which do you prefer?

Tribunal

The Christ-of-Midnight is the same as the Christ-of-Noonday (Acts 1:11; Rev. 1:17-18). But with a difference! No longer the Man of Sorrows. No longer despised and rejected of men. No longer the humble Servant. For all things have become new (Rev. 21:5). God will judge the world through his appointed sovereign Judge (John 5:27; Eph. 1:22; Acts 17:31). What stronger incentive is there to repentance, once the language of love falls on deaf ears! What more urgent summons to conversion!

For each man there is a personal judgment at the moment his life runs out. But beyond this we also catch a glimpse in Scripture of this awesome public tribunal in the End, when God will openly vindicate his grace and glory. Then He will right all wrongs and show for all the world to see that "though the wrong seems oft so strong, God is the Ruler yet." Then too, no longer looking through a glass darkly, we will fully realize that the Christian life really makes sense. Does it pay to deny yourself, take up the cross of self-sacrifice, and follow Christ in kingdom service? In that Day the answer will come through strong and clear: "Enter into the joy of thy Lord!"

This Judge never uses a double standard. The standard of right and wrong in effect now will also count then, namely, the law and the gospel. But He measures fairly. Each man will be judged by the light of revelation he possessed. Those "without the law" (Rom. 2:12-15) will be judged "without the law," that is, without the written law, but by "the law written in their hearts." Having the gospel, woe to us if we neglect so great salvation!

The Light of the World shone in Capernaum and Bethsaida, and they chose darkness instead. Therefore in the judgment it will be more tolerable for Tyre and Sidon, Sodom and Gomorrah, than for the cities of Galilee, for these pagan cities sinned against a lesser light.

The standard then, as now, is faith and obedience (works of faith). For each man will be judged according to what he has done in the body, whether good or evil (II Cor. 5:10). Hear the Judge say to those on his right hand, "Come near, ye blessed of my Father, inherit the kingdom prepared for you from the foundation of the world, for when I was hungry, and thirsty,

and estranged, and naked, and sick, and imprisoned, you minis-
tered to Me." But we reply: "When, where, how, Lord? We
have never met Thee!" Still He will answer: "Inasmuch as you
did it to one of the least of these my brethren, you did it unto
Me."

Trust and obey, for there's no other way. . . .

8. In what ways will Christ be the same at his second coming as
compared to his first coming, and in what ways will He be different?

9. Is it right to call men to conversion by warning them of the
judgment to come?

10. How will the final judgment serve to vindicate God's grace and
glory?

11. How will it vindicate the rightness of the Christian life?

12. Is it true that men will be judged by the light of revelation
which they received? What is the importance of this for non-
Christian peoples?

Life Everlasting — (32)

Variations on the Theme

Life is not a blind alley. History is not a dead-end street. The world has one final, unending Date to keep, when Christ shall be all in all.

This is the thrust of that climactic note which the church echoes weekly in its confession, "I believe the resurrection of the body and the life everlasting."

What can we say of this eternal sabbath? We see it as in a mirror, dimly (ancient mirrors were wavy and vague), and certainly the half has not been told us. Eye hath not seen and ear hath not heard, neither hath it entered into man's heart, the glories that await us (Heidelberg Catechism, Answer 58). What is heaven? And what is its terrible counterpart, hell?

Poetic voices have played romantically on these themes. Emily Dickinson leaves us these lines:

> I never spoke with God,
> Nor visited in heaven;
> Yet certain am I of the spot
> As though a chart were given.

John Greenleaf Whittier, snowbound, tries to pierce the curtain between time and eternity with these lines:

> Alas for him who never sees
> The stars shine through his cypress trees;
> Who hopeless lays his dead away,
> Nor looks to see the breaking day
> Across the mournful marbles play.

Dante's myth, *Inferno*, dwells at great lengths on a speculative view of hell. John Milton in his *Paradise Regained* offers a highly

153

imaginative picture of heaven. Sentimental hymn-writers mis-
lead many with their religious ditties about a "beautiful isle of
somewhere."

Our only reliable guide is to try to read aright what is written
in the Word. Its view of heaven is overpowering because of the
blinding brilliance of this place of "light unapproachable." Hell
too is mysterious because of its total blackout, the place of
"outer darkness." We can only skirt the outer limits of both, and
look on from a distance as Scripture points the way.

1. How would you evaluate the poetic insights mentioned above?

2. Why does the Bible describe the life of heaven as a "sabbath
   rest" (Heb. 4:9)?

3. What should we learn from Luke 16:19-31?

Grand Perspectives

In modern times liberalism has popularized the theme of a
heaven on earth. An evolutionary, optimistic, utopian illusion!
But the crises of the twentieth century have knocked the props
from under such man-made paradises. Now the fear runs high
that man will bring the End upon himself through the un-
leashing of uncontrollable nuclear reactions, reducing our world
to a radioactive shambles and wiping civilization off the face of
the globe.

Scripture, however, leads us to believe that only the almighty
intervention of God's hand in history is capable of ushering in the
great New World. This is still "my Father's world." He has not
relaxed his hold upon his handiwork. Redemption is aimed not
at snatching a few people out of the world, but ultimately at
redeeming the world itself with a redeemed mankind. God is
at work already now, and one Day will renew his creation —
not by destroying the Old Order, but by purging it, thus escalat-
ing it dramatically into the New Order. The dross will be
consumed and the gold refined.

Therefore, what we are doing here and now in our daily vocations, our total Christian service, counts heavily, both for time
and for eternity. The kingdom that will one day fully come is
now already on the way. And we are part of its program.

Luther was once planting some peach trees in his backyard.
A parishioner, coming by, thinking a minister could better

spend his time on "spiritual matters," chided him with the re-
mark, "Dr. Luther, what would you be doing today if you knew
Christ were returning tomorrow?" To which the reformer replied that he would continue planting peach trees, for they
could then become part of the New Earth.

An elderly retired Christian, avid gardener, was troubled by
his lack of intense longing for heaven. Did he feel too much at
home with God among his flowers? He shared his thoughts with
his minister, who suggested that the desire might grow if he
remembered that there would probably be room for gardeners in
the new Paradise too, just as in the original Paradise.

The point is this: there is real continuity from this world
to the next, continuity with a difference: this world renewed
and glorified.

Too often we think of this eschatological Future as something
"out of this world." We have not the slightest idea what to expect,
and consequently hardly even want it. Who really appreciates
the utterly foreign? Perhaps we need a more "worldly" view of
the New Creation. Such is certainly the language of the Bible.
It speaks of a city, with streets and a river and trees. What
should we think of? This: Chicago, Madison Avenue, Grand
River, and maple trees. *This* world renewed! All things new!

It is instructive to note that history begins with a *garden,*
Eden, and ends with a *city,* the New Jerusalem. God's grand
finale gathers up into it the products of man's cultural mandate.
Nothing good goes to waste. Therefore, get on with Christian
education, Christian social action, and every form of Christian
witness.

God will also carry *us* along in his plan. In this my flesh
shall I see God (Job 19:2). The ground for this hope is Christ.
The *same* Christ who was crucified and buried also arose (John
20:27), appeared to Paul on the Damascus Road (Acts 22:8)
and to John on Patmos (Rev. 1:18), and will come again
(Acts 1:11). This is the redemptive preview of what resurrection
will mean for us.

The body buried is the same body which will be resurrected.
The very seed sown is the same seed raised (I Cor. 15:36-38).
Christ is the perfect Savior, redeeming our whole selfhood. In
the New World we will hold the same ID cards. But with a
wonderful dimension of difference — incorruptible, glorified.

Since the whole Christian man is God's redeemed possession, here and now enlist yourself among "the pure in *spirit*" (Matt. 5:8) and "present your *bodies* a living sacrifice" (Rom. 12:1).

Because we, in the weakness of faith, often struggle with the question of the resurrection of the body, Calvin notes that "Scripture provides two helps by which to overcome this great obstacle: one in the parallel of Christ's resurrection, and the other in the omnipotence of God" (*Institutes,* III, 25, 3).

4. How has the heaven-on-earth theme been expressed by certain thinkers in our times?

5. Explain both the continuity and the discontinuity between the present life and the future life.

6. Do you agree with the words of Luther and the words of the pastor given above?

7. Why does the Bible introduce the New World as a city?

8. How are we to understand our resurrection in the light of Christ's resurrection?

Heaven and Hell

At the end of history there are just two exits, hell and heaven. Between them is fixed an unbridgeable gulf (Luke 16:26). Then the antithesis will be final and absolute. What can we say about these two realms?

Both are the ultimate end-products of the choices men make in this life. Now already we experience a foretaste of both, as Rev. J. Overduin points out in his book, *Heaven and Hell in Dachau.* What the full realities will be, only time will tell. Nothing in this life, not even the most beautiful evening gown, can really be called "heavenly." And it is high time we de-glamorize hell. For war may be "hellish," but never really hell.

Two things at least stand out about hell. First, it is the place of inexpressible *loneliness*, total alienation from God, and total fragmentation of human relations. Rugged individualism! C. S. Lewis describes hell as a place where men forever just hang around, pulling at their hair, trying desperately to recall a Name they had heard long ago, a Name that offered hope — but unable to remember it! Every man is an island! Second, hell is the place of perpetual *unemployment*. Nothing to do, nowhere to go. Deadening treadmill. Time hanging heavy on their hands. Heaven is the happy counterpart. It offers the full life, family style, in the Father's house. The marriage feast of the Lamb. Holy laughter, with every tear wiped away. And undergirding it all, perfect *fellowship* with our Lord and the full communion of the people of God. Also, the new earth under new heavens offers opportunities unlimited to go places and do things. A place for co-workers to carry on constructive *activities*, singing while we work, and every day new horizons to conquer.

No wonder a Christian father, gathered with his family around the Sunday meal, exclaimed: "All this, and heaven too!"

9. How can our Sundays be a foretaste of the eternal sabbath?

10. What signs of heaven and hell are evident already in this life?

11. What main points would you include in a comparison of heaven and hell?

GLOSSARY

In the interest of better understanding, this Glossary offers an (all too) brief clarification of some of the more technical theological terminology found in the book.

THE DOCTRINE OF SCRIPTURE

INSPIRATION is the overruling guidance of the Holy Spirit in the historical process of writing the Bible, whereby He so moved the authors of the books of the Bible — in accordance with the background, training, culture, and temperament of each writer — that sovereignly, yet freely, they were led to transcribe divine revelation in harmony with the intent and purpose of God the Revealer.

INFALLIBILITY is that quality of Scripture which expresses Christian confidence in the trustworthy, reliable, and non-deceptive character of the Word of God as an inerrant and unfailing revelation of God's will for our lives.

AUTHORITY is that comprehensive mark of Scripture which expresses Christian faith in the binding and normative power of the Word of God in our lives, calling us in an ongoing fashion to discerning and obedient response in all our thoughts, words, and deeds.

CANONICITY is a theological concept which covers that historical process whereby Scripture, through its self-authenticating power, established for itself an undisputed place in the believing heart of the church as the supreme rule ("canon") for faith and life.

TRANSMISSION is that divinely provident, Spirit-led process by which the church was guided in transcribing the original books of the Bible (the autographa) into numerous copies (the manuscripts), and then translating them into various languages (the versions of the Bible) so that God's Word was made available to men in various times and places.

INTERPRETATION (HERMENEUTICS) is that ongoing, disciplined activity of the Christian community by which it has sought to understand clearly God's Word and apply it in

Christian living by following sound rules of biblical exegesis.

THE TEXT OF SCRIPTURE

THE SEPTUAGINT is the classic translation of the Old Testament from the Hebrew into the Greek language among Greek-speaking Jews in dispersion during the inter-testamental period.

THE APOCRYHAL BOOKS (APOCRYPHA) are a collection of about fifteen which arose among the Jews in dispersion and gained popularity among them during the inter-testamental period (the time between Malachi and Matthew). The Apocrypha contain various literary types: history, biography, poetry, legend, devotions, and prophecy — all designed to urge the Jews to holy patriotism and loyalty to the faith of their fathers. Protestants generally do not regard them as part of the Bible (as reflected in the name "apocryphal," meaning "hidden" or "concealed"), whereas Roman Catholicism does regard them as canonical in a secondary sense.

THE VULGATE is the venerable translation of the Old Testament (Hebrew) and the New Testament (Greek) into the Latin language by Jerome, a church father who lived in the latter part of the fourth century. This translation then became the undisputed Bible of the Middle Ages and remained the authorized version of the Roman Catholic Church down to modern times.

BIBLICAL-THEOLOGICAL CONCEPTS

REVELATION signifies the mighty acts of God in making himself known to man, both through "general revelation" in creation and through "special revelation" in Scripture — and supremely in Jesus Christ.

RELIGION is a person or community's total way of life, rooted in a basic faith commitment and fundamental life principles as these come to expression in every area of human endeavor. It embraces more than prayer, devotions, and worship. It involves man as a whole in all his life relationships, the total life pattern by which confession is translated into conduct, both privately and publicly.

COVENANT is that biblical concept which describes our total life situation as creatures of God, defining our relationship of response in faith and obedience to God, which in turn defines our relationships to our fellow men and the world around us, and thus lays the basis for an all-encompassing Christian way of life.

CULTURAL MANDATE refers to that full-orbed and many-sided task which God gave to man as his crown-creature, vice-gerent, and servant in the world to "subdue the earth and have dominion over it."

WORLD-AND-LIFE VIEW is that total perspective in terms of which a person or community seeks to give concrete and practical expression to basic Christian principles both in thought and in action in every area of life.

ANTHROPOMORPHISMS are revelational literary devices in the Bible which reflect God's condescending manner in revealing himself to us by using human traits to describe himself, for example: "the arm of the Lord is not shortened," "the mouth of the Lord hath spoken," "the eyes of the Lord run to and fro through the whole earth".

ESCHATOLOGY is that section of Christian doctrine which explores biblical teachings concerning the "last things," such themes as the second coming of Christ, the final resurrection, divine judgment, and life eternal.

MILLENNIALISM deals with various Christian views concerning the "thousand years" in the Book of Revelation. Some hold to premillennialism (belief that Christ's return will usher in a thousand years of kingly rule upon earth), others to postmillennialism (belief that the kindom will be ushered in as a result of man's cultural achievements upon earth, and still others to amillennialism (that the thousand years represent the full period of time from the first to the second coming of Christ).

ORIENTATIONAL CONCEPTS

CREEDS (CONFESSIONS) are articles of faith adopted by the historic Christian church as touchstones of right doctrine and right living, in response to doctrinal and moral crises in the Christian community. Their authority and normative function in matters of Christian faith and practice rest upon their faithfulness in representing the truth of Scripture amid urgent needs in the life of the church. Creeds, therefore, serve as expressions of Christian unity, as a witness to the world, and as a standard by which to preserve orthodoxy in belief and practice.

PREACHING is that central task of the church, as prescribed in Scripture, to proclaim the gospel in all simplicity and power to all men everywhere, opening the Word in such a way that its hearers are clearly confronted with God's will for their lives and find its message meaningful for daily living.

THEOLOGY is a scholarly enterprise carried on within the Christian community in a somewhat systematic and "scientific" way, by which thinking Christians seeks to discover the doctrinal implications of their faith for living the Christian life in the world around us. For theology to be Christian it must be pursued within a biblical perspective and within the framework of the Christian creeds. This book, for example, may aptly be regarded as a kind of popular study of Christian theology.

BIBLICAL CRITICISM is a scholarly analysis of the text of the Bible which attempts to answer questions about the authorship, composition, style, time, and place of the writing of the books of the Bible. Sometimes such study is carried on in believing response to the Bible as divine revelation, and sometimes on the assumption that the Bible is a collection of purely human religious writings.

HISTORICAL SOURCES

THE APOSTLES' CREED is the classic confession of virtually all of Christendom, which probably started as a simple trinitarian affirmation and then over a period of about three or four centuries was gradually expanded to include additional elements of the Christian faith, until it finally attained its present form about the fifth century.

THE NICENE CREED is an early Christian statement of faith related to the Council of Nicea A.D. 325 which is similar in structure and content to the Apostles' Creed, in which the church defines its beliefs in the trinity and especially in Jesus Christ as truly God and truly man.

THE ATHANASIAN CREED is an early Christian statement of faith, popularly though erroneously attributed to the church father Athanasius, whose ideas it embraces, in which the church defines its beliefs in the trinity and in the person of Christ.

THE BELGIC CONFESSION is a creed divided into thirty-seven articles written by Guido de Bres in 1561 and adopted by the Reformed church of the Low Lands as an expression of their Christian faith in the face of a severe Roman Catholic counter-reformational movement.

THE HEIDELBERG CATECHISM is doubtless the most ecumenical of the sixteenth-century Reformational creeds. It was written in Germany in 1563 by two young churchmen, Ursinus and Olevianus, as an attempt to give a united witness by the Lutheran and Calvinist churches to their newly rediscovered, historic Christian faith. It was drafted in the form of questions and answers and is divided into three main parts: man's sin and misery, our redemption through Christ, and the call to grateful Christian living.

THE CANONS OF DORT is a confessional statement adopted by the Reformed churches at the Synod of Dort (1618-19) emphasizing the sovereignty of God in man's salvation over against the challenge of Arminianism.

THE CHURCH ORDER is a kind of constitution drafted by the Reformed churches at the Synod of Dort (1618-19), outlining biblical guidelines for ordering the life of the church.

THE INSTITUTES OF THE CHRISTIAN RELIGION is the rather large handbook on Christian theology written by John Calvin, published in its definitive edition in 1559. For centuries, even to the present, it has been honored as a classic statement of the Reformation faith amid the struggles of the sixteenth century.

SCHOOLS OF THOUGHT

ROMAN CATHOLICISM is that complex of beliefs and practices which are characteristic of the Roman Catholic community, both in its official doctrines and in its popular practices, taking into account the long-standing traditions coming up out of the early church through medieval times to the present, as well as the more recent impetus toward renewal.

LUTHERANISM is that branch of the Protestant Reformation movement which followed the theology of Martin Luther (d. 1546), placing a central emphasis on the doctrine of justification by faith and the priesthood of all believers.

ZWINGLIANISM is that branch of the Protestant Reformation movement which was launched in Switzerland by Ulrich Zwingli (d. 1531) and carried on by Heinrich Bullinger (d. 1575). It was generally true to the central thrust of the Reformation, but with some close relationship to the humanist Renaissance of the sixteenth century.

CALVINISM is that branch of the Protestant Reformation movement which followed the theological leadership of John Calvin (d. 1564), with its central emphasis on the sovereignty of God in all of life.

ANABAPTISM is that wing of the Protestant Reformation movement which arose in various countries in reaction against some of the more firmly established positions of the Reformation, insisting on re-baptism for adult converts, and manifesting some radical spiritualistic tendencies for Christian conduct within the church and in the world at large.

DEISM is that system of beliefs and practices which absolutizes the transcendence of God in such a way that human life and all of history are regarded as being independent of divine involvement, except for a few "miracles," thus conceiving of all earthly life as subject to purely "natural laws".

ATHEISM is a way of life erected on the assumption that there is no God, or, if ever there was a God, that now "God is dead". Though there are relatively few theoretical atheists, practical atheism (living as though God does not count in everyday life·) slays its ten thousands.

SECULARISM is that way of life so common in our Western World which seeks to divide all things into "sacred" and "secular" affairs. The "sacred" are those things supposedly related to God and faith and the church, things which must be kept personal and private. The "secular" is the public sector of life, from which "religion" must be excluded on the premise that in education, labor, politics, etc. all things are "neutral".

MODERN LIBERALISM is a nineteenth- and twentieth-century movement within Protestant Christianity which brought about a radical and total reconstruction of the historic Christian faith in the name of the "assured results" of the scientific method and in the interest of accommodating the gospel to the rationalistic demands of the so-called "modern-mind."

FUNDAMENTALISM is a typically American version of Christianity which emerged around the turn of this century. It reaffirmed certain "fundamentals" of the historic Christian faith and championed orthodox Christianity in the face of a prevailing liberal theology. To overcome some of its earlier reactionary theology, Fundamentalists today tend to prefer the more positive name "Evangelicals".

BARTHIANISM is that brand of contemporary theology which is generally characterized as "dialectical theology" and which is usually called Neo-Orthodoxy, sometimes Neo-Modernism. It emerged strongly after World War I under the leadership of the Swiss theologian, Karl Barth, who led this movement in strong reaction to classic modern liberalism and gave it a definitive formulation in his *Church Dogmatics*.

COMMUNISM is a nineteenth- and twentieth-century philosophy of life first spelled out by Marx, Engels, and Lenin, which has now taken deep root in Russia and China. It is basically atheistic in religion, exploits the idea of class struggle, is generally opposed to capitalism and a free enterprise economy, and seems bent politically on world revolution along the lines of its dialectical materialism.